T0326244

Elements in the Renaissance
edited by
John Henderson
Birkbeck, University of London and Wolfson College,
University of Cambridge
Jonathan K. Nelson
Syracuse University Florence

THE FRENCH DISEASE
IN RENAISSANCE ITALY

Representation and Experience

John Henderson
University of London
University of Cambridge

CAMBRIDGE
UNIVERSITY PRESS

Shaftesbury Road, Cambridge CB2 8EA, United Kingdom

One Liberty Plaza, 20th Floor, New York, NY 10006, USA

477 Williamstown Road, Port Melbourne, VIC 3207, Australia

314–321, 3rd Floor, Plot 3, Splendor Forum, Jasola District Centre, New Delhi – 110025, India

103 Penang Road, #05–06/07, Visioncrest Commercial, Singapore 238467

Cambridge University Press is part of Cambridge University Press & Assessment, a department of the University of Cambridge.

We share the University's mission to contribute to society through the pursuit of education, learning and research at the highest international levels of excellence.

www.cambridge.org
Information on this title: www.cambridge.org/9781009507530

DOI: 10.1017/9781009236317

First published 2024

A catalogue record for this publication is available from the British Library.

ISBN 978-1-009-50753-0 Hardback
ISBN 978-1-009-23633-1 Paperback
ISSN 2631-9101 (online)
ISSN 2631-9098 (print)

The French Disease in Renaissance Italy

Representation and Experience

Elements in the Renaissance

DOI: 10.1017/9781009236317
First published online: December 2024

John Henderson
University of London
University of Cambridge

Author for correspondence: John Henderson, jh101@cam.ac.uk

Abstract: This Element provides a fresh approach to the representation and experience of the French Disease, by reassessing a wide range of textual and visual sources through the lens of contemporary medical ideas. It analyses how knowledge about the Great Pox was transmitted to a literate and also a wider public through performance and the circulation of popular prints. Chronicles, satirical and moralistic poems and plays about prostitutes, along with autobiographical accounts, described symptoms and the experience of patients, reflecting how non-medical men and women understood the nature of this terrible new disease and its profound physical and psychological impact. The second major theme is how the French Disease was represented visually. Woodcuts and broadsheets showing the moral and physical decline of courtesans are analysed together with graphic medical illustrations of symptoms and their treatment together with images of the diseased body of St Job, patron saint of the French Disease.

This Element also has a video abstract: www.cambridge.org/EREN_Henderson

Keywords: Renaissance Italy, the French Disease, visualising disease, patient experience, literature and sickness

ISBNs: 9781009507530 (HB), 9781009236331 (PB), 9781009236317 (OC)
ISSNs: 2631-9101 (online), 2631-9098 (print)

Contents

Introduction

Figure 1, a vivid image of a middle-aged, bearded man covered with the spots and lesions of the French Disease or the Great Pox, is the first of a series of twenty-seven watercolours in a late sixteenth-century album in the Biblioteca Augusta in Perugia (MS G61). Each of these watercolours was designed to demonstrate the effects of disease on the body of a patient and the treatment prescribed by practitioners, many of whom were surgeons and who appeared in the following pages.

The patient is shown dressed in a loose garment to retain his modesty and at the same time reveals the effects of the disease from which he suffered. His face shows a prominent red sore, and ulcers cover his hands, chest, legs and feet. There is also evidence of larger darker brown ulcerated patches around his knees and further discolouration of the skin appears on his groin under his shift. As with most of the images in this album, the man reveals something of his character and reactions. He is suffering from very itchy sores, since he scratches his chest with his right hand. At the same time, his expression suggests a patient resignation, as he sits in front of a roaring fire and submits to heat treatment to sweat out the poison of disease. A mug in the foreground may contain a sudorific drink, such as Holy Wood or Guaiacum, regarded as the new wonder drug, which was seen as a cure when more traditional remedies failed.

It was the immediacy of this and other images in the album which convinced me to return to the history of this disease in Renaissance Italy (Arrizabalaga, Henderson, French, 1997 [cited as AHF]; cf. Zanca, 1984). This little-known album appears to be almost unique for the visual detail of the disease's impact on the human body, for, to date, no illustrated medical treatises on the Pox have been identified for Renaissance Italy. However, little is known about the provenance of the Perugian album. It may have formed part of the original collection of books and manuscripts which Prospero Podiani donated to the city in 1582, and which formed the nucleus of the Biblioteca Augusta. He was interested in medicine; his uncle was an eminent physician, and he might have bought the manuscript in Padua, where he frequented the medical school (Panzanelli Fratoni, 2012; Bartoli Langeli, Panzanelli Fratoni, 2016).[1] His interest in the French Disease may also have gone beyond the watercolour album, since the library contains three copies of the 1556 Italian treatise on the disease by Pietro Rostinio.

The album may also have been commissioned by a medical practitioner or medical corporation in Perugia, and then sold subsequently. There was considerable local interest in the French Disease (Mal Francese), reflected in the foundation in 1585 by the hospitaller Order of San Giovanni di Dio of the

---

[1] The earliest reference to the album in the library was in the 1634 inventory of the librarian, Ludovico Aureli: 'Figure diverse di malfrancesati'.

Figure 1 Pox patient sweating (late sixteenth century), (Biblioteca Communale Augusta Perugia (BCAP), (MS G61, c. 4r)

Incurabili hospital of S. Niccolò specialising in incurable diseases (Stroppiana, 1968). In the same period, the University of Perugia established its first chair of anatomy and surgery, and the first holder of the position was the celebrated professor from Padua, Pietro Paolo Galera (Maovaz et al., 2008, 280–1; Lupi, 2014). The album may therefore have had a series of potential functions from the self-promotion of the expertise of a surgeon, as a guide to the symptoms and treatment of the French Disease for those working in the Incurabili hospital or teaching in the university.

The anonymous manuscript remains an enigma, since it contains no text, and following the twenty-seven illustrations, the remaining ninety-nine folios are blank (Barlozzini, 2009, scheda 36). Without any external verification about who might have commissioned the album or even where, one can only rely on internal iconographic evidence to suggest its function. My initial assumption was that it had been commissioned to illustrate a treatise, and indeed, as with contemporary pathological illustrations, the album suggests collaboration between the artist and a medical practitioner (Bertoloni Meli, 2017, 16). However, there is no obvious match to existing works on the Great Pox and, while most of the plates are related to the disease, there are at least seven generic images probably representing other medical conditions. Furthermore, the water-colours do not appear to have been conceived as a whole, for they were done by three different hands. The first three images, representing the severe symptoms of male patients, were framed by a cornice and had been drawn and coloured on separate paper, from where they had been cut out and glued into the Perugia album. The second group consists of nine images of mostly young men on pedestals, in various stages of the disease. Then only half of the last fifteen images, more amateur watercolours of larger figures, can definitely be linked to the Pox (Barlozzini, 2009, scheda 36, 29).

The Perugian manuscript may have been unique in Italy in its detailed representation of the French Disease, but its form is part of wider genre of albums which emerged from the later sixteenth century, from costume books to collections of botanical illustrations to friendship books. What they all had in common, whether in manuscript or print, was that they were illustrated, even if with different functions. Those representing dress linked a discussion of cos-tumes with customs of sometimes faraway countries such as the Ottoman Empire and Japan; botanical books were, as their name implies, illustrations of native and exotic plants with their medicinal properties; while friendship books contained a wide variety of texts and illustrations from signatures and poems to descriptions and depictions of places and individuals which the compiler had encountered on their travels (Wilson, 2005, ch. 2; Rublack, 2010; Kusukawa, 2012; Calvi, 2022).

All these authors shared a common curiosity, whether in the appearance of the natural work or human beings. The Perugian album was, then, part of this wider movement to record and understand the world around them and the human body, building on the booming field of anatomical illustration. But though that period saw the growth in the publication of works written by surgeons across Europe, including those of Ambrose Paré and Guido Guidi, and Giovanni Della Croce, the illustrations were very different from those in the Perugian album. Woodcuts detailing surgical procedures tended to emphasise the importance of the role of instruments and procedures rather than diseased states. In contrast to the very human reactions of patients in the Perugian watercolours, surgical works often show blank expressions, even when under-going major surgery. One of the few contemporary surgical treatises to show details of symptoms on the human body is the 1517 *Feldbüch der Wundartzney* (*Fieldbook of Surgery*) by the military surgeon Hans von Gesdorff, but a leprous patient was still represented in a very schematic way as an object of inspection than a subject with emotions (Bertoloni Meli, 2017, 16–26). Furthermore, the patients illustrated in the roughly contemporary manuscript to the Fugger hospital in Augsburg show little reaction when undergoing the painful operation for the removal of the bladder stone, for which this institution was famous (Kinzelbach and Weber, 2022).

Further studies may reveal more about the context which led to the commissioning of the Perugian album and possible influences and models for the figures. The mannered gestures of the nudes suggest they may have been based on illustrations of sculptures, as was the case with an Italian mid sixteenth-century album of watercolours in the British Museum. They depicted a wide variety of subjects illustrating classical, biblical and medical subjects, some of which have been identified as having been copied from sixteenth-century botanical and anatomical books.[2] However, even without further identification the vivid images of the Perugian album add a very human dimension to our discussion by their detailed visual representation of symptoms and treatment, placing patients at centre stage.

This interdisciplinary study examines how the French Disease was viewed and experienced at the time through its reinterpretation of a range of textual and visual sources from a medical point of view. Emphasis will be placed on how the disease was understood at the time to gauge better the reactions and perceptions of contemporaries. As we shall see in Section 1, the disease was known by a number of labels,[3] most common of which was the French Disease, which subsequent historians have tended to identify it with syphilis. The term had a Renaissance connotation through a poem of the same name written in about 1530 by the well-known Veronese physician, Girolamo Fracastoro. He also published a Latin treatise on contagious diseases, *De contagion*, in about 1546, in which he referred to the 'French Disease' rather than syphilis, a term which only came into general use many centuries later. Indeed, how far the sixteenth-century disease can be identified as the same as that common to the nineteenth or twentieth centuries remains a matter of debate. On the one hand, as in the case of many illnesses, contemporaries noted that it had mutated after thirty years, becoming less acute and furthermore developed three distinct phases. On the other hand, recent osteo-archaeological research has revealed the presence of treponemal diseases, of which syphilis is one, in the bones of medieval skeletons, well before the date when historians have believed the disease first appeared in Europe with the return of Columbus from the Americas. While the investigation of the pre-history of the disease is a fascinating and productive field, it is less central to this Element, which deals with when it became

---

[2] British Museum 197*.d.2. I am grateful to Sarah Vowles of the Department of Prints and Drawings, and also Pat Rubin and Chris Fischer for their invaluable comments and suggestions concerning the Perugian album.

[3] The following terms will be used interchangeably in what follows: the French Disease, Mal Francese, the Great Pox.

epidemic and spread rapidly through Europe (AHF, ch. 1; Carmichael, 1990; Stein, 2009, ch. 1; Stolberg, 2021; Salmon, 2022).

This Element goes beyond an analysis of medical treatises to examine a wide variety of written and visual sources. Some of these are relatively well-known to specialists in the field, and I shall be building on their work to provide an integrated discussion of the wider social and cultural impact of the French Disease on Renaissance Italy. Only recently have scholars begun to take seriously how sixteenth-century chronicles, satirical poems and plays, diaries and letters, reflected and interpreted medical ideas about the disease and its effects (Shemek, 2004; Ciccarella, 2018–19; Henderson, 2021a; Strocchia and Kelly, 2022; Gagné, forthcoming). Another important theme of this study is the visual representation of the Great Pox. While there are individual studies of aspects of this topic, there is no comprehensive survey of this broad range of mediums from cheap prints accompanying satirical poems and broadsheets to medical illustrations to images of St Job as patron saint of the Great Pox (Kurz, 1952; Kunzle, 1973; Terrien, 1996; Carnevale, 2010, 2015; Lodone, 2015).

If historians have tended to examine the Great Pox from the perspective of their own discipline, this study presents a broader, more integrated understanding of the experience of society and the individual with this devastating epidemic. I shall begin with a summary of the initial reactions of contemporary lay, non-medical writers, as reflected in the records of chroniclers, as they sought to understand how to cope with its effects on both the public and private spheres. The survival of some thirty chronicles, mostly from northern and central Italy, many dating from within the first ten years of the outbreak of the disease, makes it possible to gauge the reactions across a wide range of society from masons and tanners to bishops and papal secretaries.

One theme which emerges in these chronicles was that the spread of the Pox was linked to particular groups in society, such as Jews, the Moriscoes, the poor and prostitutes (Foa, 1990). Whole nations were blamed, hence the appellation Mal Francese or Morbus Gallicus, for the French were believed to have imported the disease, when King Charles VIII invaded in 1494. The French used the term 'Mal de Naples'; they claimed their soldiers had contracted it there, since the disease had spread there from Spain because of the Kingdom's very close association with Spain through politics and trade (Foa, 1990; Quétel, 1990, 16; Cohn, 2018, 97–106; Falcucci, 2020).

Medical ideas about the nature, transmission and treatment of the Great Pox (Section 2) provide the lens through which to examine its written and visual representation. From the early debates about its identity, sixteenth-century doctors wrote treatises describing its symptoms in increasing detail, developing new ideas about transmission and new therapies. This rapid survey of how

Italian medical experts understood what they called Mal Francese will help us to comprehend the ways lay contemporaries portrayed the disease. It also helps explain why certain courses of treatment were prescribed by medical practitioners, from mercury, heat, sweating and Guaicum. The section will end by asking how far these descriptions of treatment were translated into practice by examining its representation in the Perugian album, and descriptions of actual practice through petitions of practitioners to medical colleges for licences to treat the Great Pox. In this way we shall come closer to understanding how a range of actors viewed the disease, from physicians, surgeons and women empirics to hospital administrators, providing a context within which to examine the patient's reactions in the following sections.

The ensuing sections investigate the diffusion and readership of medical ideas, their influence on the language of the authors of poems, plays and images, for, as has been observed for early modern France, the Great Pox crossed many literary genres (Losse, 2015, 5–6). Medical texts and ideas will be used as a point of reference to explicate the representation of the disease across a wide range of written sources, emphasising how basic ideas of Galenic medicine were spread throughout society, reflected in the popularity of advice literature, *Regimina Sanitatis*, and recipe collections in early modern Europe (Pomata, 1998; Leong, 2008; Cavallo and Storey, 2013, 2017). Many of the authors of the poems and plays and chapbooks would probably have been familiar with these more popular medical texts, and thus humoural theory and treatment. The central question to be addressed is how far these non-medical texts reflected contemporary medical understanding of the Great Pox, as an increasing number of treatises were written or translated into the vernacular, including those by Niccolò Massa (1524), Leonardo Fioravanti (1564) and Pietro Rositini (1556). In the case of Fracastoro himself, both his poem *Syphilis* of 1530 and his treatise *De contagione* (1546) were written in Latin, the former providing the germ of his ideas developed sixteen years later.

Section 3 examines the experience of Pox patients in Renaissance Italy building on the approaches and findings of recent studies of northern and southern Europe, including Toledo, Venice, Augsburg and Nuremburg and London (Siena, 2005; Stein, 2006, 2009; Berco, 2011, 2016; McGough, 2011; O'Brien, 2019). They reflect an emerging historiography prioritising the agency and experience of patients, in contrast to a more traditional focus on official medical practitioners. While in Italy historians have examined a range of these ego documents, most famously the colourful poems and letters by Agnolo Firenzuola and Pietro Aretino, less attempt has been made to assess their descriptions of their symptoms and treatment through contemporary medical understanding. We examine the diary of a canon of Orvieto Cathedral, Ser

Tommaso di Silvestro in the 1490s; letters of Francesco Gonzaga in Mantua; works of satirists, such as Niccolò Campani of Siena and Maestro Andrea Veneziano, both associated with the papal court; and the goldsmith Benvenuto Cellini's autobiographical account of his brush with Mal Francese in the 1530s. Although many are self-consciously literary works, they reveal much about the personal suffering of Pox patients, as do the Perugian watercolours.

Satirical literature associated with prostitution provides the basis for Section 4. Poems and plays, such as Maestro Andrea's *Il Purgatorio delle Cortigiane* of 1529 (*The Purgatory of the Courtesans*) multiplied over the sixteenth century through cheaply produced leaflets and chapbooks, as did broadsheets illustrating the rise and decline of poxed prostitutes.[4] Much attention has been paid to the wider social and moralistic themes behind this literature, with its emphasis on the blame attributed to fallen women and the alleged overweening social and intellectual pretensions of courtesans, but less on how this literature and accompanying imagery reflected the way Pox and its treatment were understood by non-medical writers (in addition to the authors already cited, see Matthews Grieco, 1997; Storey, 2008; Ugolini, 2009; Geschwind, 2012; cf. on early modern England Fabricius, 1994; Healy, 2001).

The final section examines the representation of the Great Pox in contemporary Italian painting through images of St Job as patron saint of the disease. There are surprisingly few detailed studies of this topic, in comparison to Job's role as patron of 'leprosy', although there is a considerable debate about how far the medieval disease of 'lepra' can be identified with modern-day Hansen's Disease (Rawcliffe, 2006, ch. 1). In what follows I shall therefore refer to the disease as 'lepra', reflecting contemporary understanding of the term to cover a series of skin infections (Jacquart and Thomasset, 1985, 183–5; Rawcliffe, 2006, 72–8; Boeckl, 2011; Helas, 2018). Just as popular literature, pamphlets and broadsheets spread information about the Great Pox, so did images of St Job in northern and central Italy in a wide range of sites from chapels associated with hospitals, confraternities and parochial and mendicant churches.

By bringing together a range of written and visual evidence, this Element seeks to re-evaluate how the Great Pox was understood and impacted Italian and renaissance society both individually and collectively. Indeed, by exploring and comparing the representation and experience of a wide range of actors from chroniclers and medical writers and practitioners to the authors of satirical poems, plays and letter collections, we shall examine differences in the way these writers described the disease. This analysis privileged the point of view of

---

[4] Contemporaries used both the terms courtesan ('cortigiana') and prostitute ('meretrice').

literate men, rather than the courtesans themselves, whose lives were described or illustrated in popular pamphlets and broadsheets. A wider public would have absorbed the messages behind this popular literature at the recitation or performance of these plays and poems in marketplaces and seen broadsheets displayed in taverns. They would have learned more about the nature and effects of the Great Pox, as they did when gazing at the representation of St Job in chapels and churches across northern and central Italy.

1 Pox and Chronicles

1.1 Introduction

> Anno 1500. I should like to record a strange and horrible sickness which began in Italy in the year 1494, which I, Friano de' Ubaldini, forgot to put in its [proper chronological] order. [When] King Charles of France came to Italy, as I have said, in order to take the Kingdom of Naples, a strange and horrible sickness began to affect men and women, which was not known to any doctor. And people said that the French had carried the said sickness into Italy and gave it the name the French Disease. This sickness was of various types, which came with boils and also with pains, and few recovered; and because this sickness was long-lasting, ultimately the majority of these people died over a long period. And the said sickness was sticky like mistletoe ('chome fa el vischio') [and caught] by eating and drinking and through carnal relations, and many people who caught this sickness were never seen again and remained crippled and starved, and the bodies of many others were all eaten up with boils and pains. The hospitals did not want to receive and to house those with a similar sickness and for this reason many poor men and women did not have anywhere to go. Thus some good men of Bologna established a hospital for people with such sicknesses and began to put beds and other furnishings in the Hospital of San Lorenzo de' Guarini, and they called the hospital after Saint Job, and it was given a large amount of alms and it became full with these said poor men and women, who were diligently looked after.
>
> (Corradi, 1884, 346)

This passage from the *History of Bologna* by the haberdasher Friano degli Ubaldini is one of the more detailed descriptions of the Mal Francese written by a non-medical author. He wrote this passage some six years after the appearance of the disease, with more perspective on its impact than shorter chronicler accounts from the beginning of the epidemic.

Ubaldini outlines the themes mentioned by many of his contemporaries when recording the advent of the French Disease. It began in 1494, coinciding with the arrival of the French troops in Italy, hence the name French Disease. Ubaldini also emphasised that it was an unknown, strange and horrible sickness, which was characterised by boils and pains, and that it lasted a long time, leading to the afflicted becoming crippled with very few recovering. He recorded that citizens of Bologna had clubbed together and raised enough money to convert the existing hospital of S. Lorenzo de' Guarini into a centre for treating this sickness and other incurable diseases.

A wide range of Italian chroniclers recorded the arrival and the initial impact of the French Disease (cf. AHF, ch. 2; Foa, 1990; Tognotti, 2006, ch. 1). Many were compiled and published in 1884 by Alfonso Corradi, a tireless physician turned medical historian (AHF, ch. 1; Zanobio and Armocida, 1983). Almost all his sources were from the area between Milan and Venice in the north and Florence and Rome in the centre. Most of these chroniclers came from major cities, as did most of the archivists and librarians that Corradi had approached for information. The geographical distribution also reflects the concentration of large and medium sized cities in the Italian north and centre, to which Corradi added Naples and Palermo. In these urban conurbations, universities had been founded and doctors published treatises on the Pox, while in two cities, Bologna and Ferrara, public debates took place in the 1490s, specifically about whether the French Disease was a new disease or had been described by classical medical writers such as Galen and Hippocrates.

The chroniclers came were from a wide variety of professional backgrounds that often resist precise categorisation, ranging from papal secretary to tanner, and including priests, historians and politicians. For example, Bartolomeo Senarega, an official chronicler, who wrote the *Commentaries on the Events of the City of Genoa* from 1488 to 1514, worked as a notary, ambassador and civic administrator. By definition, chroniclers, both ecclesiastical and lay, were literate, whose livelihoods depended on expressing themselves orally and in writing. Three worked at the papal court, where cases had been identified. Two chroniclers were associated closely with Pope Julius II: the humanist and historian Raffaello Maffei da Volterra, who mentioned the Mal Francese under 1496 in his *Commentarium Urbanorum* (1506), and the papal secretary Sigismondo dei Conti da Foligno. Sigismondo's chronicle was almost co-terminus with the years of Julius's papacy, 1503–12, and the French Disease is mentioned in 1503. Later in the century, the protonotary and papal secretary, Cirillo Bernardino Aquilano (1500–75), described the advent and impact of Mal Francese in his *Annali* of Aquilea, which he finished in 1540, thus providing a longer perspective on the unfolding of the disease. This brief survey shows how the growing familiarity of urban literate classes with the Great Pox was reflected in the greater detail of chroniclers' descriptions of its nature, symptoms and mode of transmission.

The majority of these chroniclers were from cities where specialised hospitals for incurables, the Incurabili, had been established. The problem had been spelled out in Leo X's Bull *Salvatoris Nostri Domini Jesu Christi* in 1515 (AHF, 155):

[F]or a number of years, a large number of the sick poor, all infected with various kinds of incurable diseases, have come together from many parts of the world in this city. [They have come] in such great numbers that they cannot gain entrance without difficulty to the hospitals of the city, because of the multitude of such people, who are afflicted with an incurable sickness, [which] give annoyance to the sight and sense of smell, so that they are obliged to beg for their living through Rome, dragging themselves along on little carts.

The Bull underlines, as had Friano degli Ubaldini, that patients with incurable diseases such as lepra and plague were excluded from general medical hospitals. The Bull also expressed a wider concern, the threat posed by the sick through their smell and bad breath, which were seen as corrupting the air and potentially infecting those with whom they came into contact, a theme underlined by medical and lay commentators.

If Leo X was largely responsible for repurposing the hospital of San Giacomo in Rome, the majority of the Italian Incurabili had been founded through the influence of the Companies of Divine Love, whose members included some of the leading lights of the Catholic reform movement from Caterina Fieschi and Ettore Vernazza in Genoa to Filippo Neri and Gaetano Thiene in Rome. Their proselytising activities in promoting lay religious devotion and active charity inspired local secular and ecclesiastical authorities to help finance some of the largest of this type of hospital in early modern Europe. By 1530 some ten new Incurabili had been founded in Italy as well as specialised wards in existing hospitals, a pattern repeated, though often on a smaller scale in countries such as Germany, France and England (AHF, ch. 7; Quétel, 1990, 64–5; Siena, 2005; Stein, 2009, 1; Falcucci, 2020). It was no accident these chroniclers mentioned the Incurabili, as they reflected policies towards those sick from the French Disease and boosted the charitable reputation of their cities.

1.2 Names and Origins

Most chroniclers, like Friano degli Ubaldini's account of the beginning of the epidemic, used a version of the phrase 'the French Disease'. In Florence the apothecary Luca Landucci called it 'French boils', and the patrician Piero di Marco Parenti referred to it as 'French scab'. Most writers attributed its rapid spread to Charles VIII's troops travelling throughout Italy, and the local women with whom they had sex, both willingly and unwillingly. Understandably, the French shifted the blame elsewhere, using 'Mal de Naples', claiming their troops contracted the disease in that city. Chroniclers across Europe blamed Mal Francese on mercenaries returning home from the Italian campaign, as mentioned, for example, by the Burgundian chronicler Jean Molinet and the Strasbourg chronicler (Quétel, 1990, 11–13; Stein, 2009, 1–2; Cohn, 2018, ch. 5).

Italian writers also knew of its Neapolitan origins, as recorded by Landucci: 'And on 11 January 1496/7, Monsignore Begni [d'Aubigny] came from Naples, with perhaps fifty horses, and he was sick. He had the French boils. He arrived in a basket. He was lodged in the house of Jacopo de' Pazzi, where he was accorded great honour' (Landucci, 1985 ed., 143). D'Aubigny, Lord Bernard Stuart, was a commander of the French army in Charles VIIII's invasion and led the French retreat. He contracted the French Disease in Naples, and had to be carried in a basket, rather than sitting astride one of his fifty horses. Significantly, in contrast to plague, which was also current in Florence in this decade, D'Aubigny's Pox was not regarded as a being threat to the health of others. As a French general, he was received by the Florentines with honours and stayed with the Pazzi, one of the leading patrician families in the city. He was next recorded in Ferrara, where he stayed with Duke Ercole d'Este. Ferrara's anonymous chronicler was particularly struck by D'Aubigny's condition; he described him as 'being ill from a certain disease called the French Disease, which causes very severe pains and hard buboes all over the body' (AHF, 44–5).

The name Mal Francese or Morbus Gallicus became the most common label not just in Italy but also in many countries in western Europe, including England and Germany (Foa, 1990; Quétel, 1990, 16; Cohn, 2018, ch. 8). Most of the first generation of Italian chroniclers were content to refer to the French as the originators of the disease, backed up by Spanish doctors working at the papal court, such as Gaspar Torrella (Arrizabalaga, 2005). Then gradually the perceived geographical origins widened; the Sicilian chronicler recorded that in 1498 the Spanish had brought it to the Kingdom of Naples from Spain, where it had in turn arrived from the New World following Columbus's return from the 'Indies' (Corradi, 1884, 347; Cohn, 2018, ch. 5; Falcucci, 2020).

The New World origins of the French Disease became more widely accepted by the second generation of Italian chroniclers. Both the protonotary and papal secretary, Cirillo Bernardino Aquilano writing in about 1540, and the historian Francesco Guicciardini writing in the late 1530s, repeated the story. The latter wrote that

> it would be just to absolve the French from this ignominy, because it is obvious that this malady had been carried to Naples from Spain; nor was it really a product of that nation either, for it had been brought there from those islands which began to be known in our hemisphere almost during those same years as a result of the voyage of Christopher Columbus, the Genoese

(Guicciardini, 1971 ed., 234). Other chronicles in Italy and elsewhere linked the Pox to specific social groups, such as Jews, Moriscoes, the poor and prostitutes, although it seems that Pox, in contrast to plague, did not lead to their persecution

(Cohn, 2018, 97–106; cf. Foa, 1990; Quétel, 1990, 16). Sigismondo dei Conti recounted that the Pox arrived from Spain when the Jews were expelled, providing a Biblical parallel for the spread of 'lepra' after the Jews were driven out of Egypt (Corradi, 1884, 365–6). Later in the sixteenth century, the surgeon and empiric Leonardo Fioravanti, ever keen to reject medical orthodoxy, dismissed the New World origins of the disease and its novelty by championing the idea of cannibalism, suggesting the Pox derived from soldiers during the Italian wars, who had been driven by starvation to eat the bodies of the dead, a theme taken up in sixteenth-century France (Eamon 1998, 10–12; Losse, 2015, ch. 3).

The attribution of labels to diseases has always been an important way of attempting to understand and control them. The Papal secretary Raffaello Maffei da Volterra reported in 1496 that it was said that the disease was either 'elephantiasis' or 'satyriasis' (Corradi, 1884, 359). Contemporaries also drew an association between the French Disease and 'lepra', one of the most common epidemic diseases in the Middle Ages, and images discussed in following sections reflect this conflation or overlap between the two diseases in the 1490s. The chronicler of Cremona even recorded that everybody who saw a person with the Great Pox thought they were lepers (Corradi, 1884, 361). Lepra also affected the skin through the eruption of ulcerated spots and lesions, and lepers had long been highly visible in medieval cities, where they were housed and treated in leprosaria. In 1496, Fileno delle Tuatte had labelled the new disease the 'lepra of Saint Job', reflecting Job's position as its patron saint, while others in Ferrara and Venice (Marin Sanudo) called it the 'sickness of San Job' (Corradi, 1884, 346). This period coincided with the continued decline of this disease, leaving the field open to the growing association of Job with the French Disease, a topic examined in Section 5 (AHF, 52–54).

1.3 Symptoms

Chroniclers across Italy and Europe presented similar descriptions of the horrifying symptoms of the French Disease. Many of the earliest chroniclers discussed the appearance of the Great Pox in more generalised terms, as when the apothecary Luca Landucci first mentioned it in his diary on 28 May 1496: 'there began a certain sickness that was called the French boils like a large pock'; and by 5 December he recorded its spread: 'And in this time, Florence and its countryside were full of French boils, as was every city in Italy, and they lasted for a long while' (Landucci, 1985 ed., 132, 141). Landucci mentioned one of the main external symptoms, the boils (*bolle*), which he likened to a 'Great Pox' ('vagiuolo grosso'), though he did not suggest it led to death, in contrast to when another disease broke out the following May: 'in this time people died of fever in this area and in the hospitals; this fever made people rant and almost lose their minds and [led to] . . . their death within two or three days' (Landucci, 1985 ed., 150). He recorded disease incidents throughout his diary to 1516, whereas only four entries mentioned the French Disease between May 1496 and January 1497. This reflects the nature of the Pox, which became a serious chronic ailment rather than a dramatic episode of acute epidemic disease, which killed rapidly. Landucci was typical of many chroniclers who recorded Mal Francese at the time it appeared. It was worthy of note when it was new, but less as it became an established part of everyday life, except when a famous person was afflicted severely or a city celebrated the foundation of an Incurabili hospital for the treatment of Mal Franciosati.

The first generation of chroniclers shared a broadly similar vocabulary when describing the symptoms, with 'boils' as the most common term used, and other local variations, including 'brozzole' and 'rogna grossa'. Many mentioned severe pains and swollen joints. As Fileno dalle Tuatte wrote, patients 'could not move from bed' (Corradi, 1884, 346), while Sigismondo dei Conti da Foligno wrote, probably based on his own observation at the papal court, that this led them 'to scream out day and night without ceasing' (Corradi, 1884, 363). The Perugian chronicler Francesco Maturanzio recorded that some suffered so much that in desperation they threw themselves into the river (Matarazzo, 1851 ed., 33).

An unusually detailed description of the symptoms of Mal Francese appears in the diary of the Venetian patrician Marin Sanudo (Sanudo, 1879 ed., I, 137):

> And by its nature it weakens the limbs, hands and feet, into a type of gout, and creates pustules and tumid blisters all over the body and on the face, with fevers and arthritic pains, so that the whole skin is full of it, on the face up to the eyes, as does smallpox (*varuole*), and in the case of women, all the limbs up to the nature [genitals], [leaving them] in such discomfort that such patients cry out for death. And as the said evil comes to the modest parts first, in the case of coitus it is contagious, otherwise not. It is said moreover that infants have it, and it lasts various lengths of time. And even though it is a very ugly disease, few then die.

Sanudo mentions the most obvious signs of the disease, the pustules and blisters all over the body, but he also emphasises their particular visibility on the face 'up to the eyes', and the pains in limbs, leading to patients wishing to die rather than to suffer any more. He links the disease to 'the modest parts', asserting that it was spread through coitus, and that it could be contracted by infants. Some idea of the impact of the disease on the body and face can be appreciated from the seventh Perugian watercolour (Figure 2), which shows a nude man half-turned away from the viewer. He is covered in red sores, as well as some more

Figure 2 Pox patient with red sores and black lesions
(late sixteenth century): (BCAP, MS G61, c. 21r)

serious black lesions. He holds out his arms crossed in front of him with his
hands extended as though in agony, illustrating Sanudo's comment 'such
patients cry out for death'.

1.4 Transmission

The question of how the French Disease was transmitted was clearly of vital
importance to medical practitioners in advising people how to avoid contracting
this 'horrible disease'. Section 2 will examine in more detail medical theories of
transmission, but chroniclers in the early stages of the epidemic recorded
a variety of explanations. Friano mentioned the risks of 'eating and drinking
and carnal relations', while Elia Cavriolo recounts that the Pox could be caught
through close proximity or even by sleeping in the same bed (Corradi, 1884,
345; Cavriolo, 1585, 214). In Florence, in 1504, deliberations of the cathedral
board of works revealed the canons' fear of contracting the French Disease from
the public. They asked for a new wooden cupboard to be constructed so that they

could keep separate 'the chasuble, chalices and liturgical vestments' used during communion (Puccinotti, 1850–66, ii/2, 505).

It is no surprise that there should have been a wide variety of explanations of how Mal Francese was spread in its early stages, given the continued debates about how even plague was transmitted 150 years after the Black Death. But a certain delicacy was also required, for ecclesiastical figures were listed among those who had caught the disease, as noted by the lawyer Francesco Muralti in his chronicle of Como: 'popes, kings, princes, marchionesses, dukes, soldiers, nearly all the nobility, merchants, and all who are lustful, and secular and regular clergy' (Corradi, 1884, 362). Even so, many chroniclers from across Italy agreed that sexual transmission was one of its main causes, whether they were from Venice, Ferrara, Bologna, Siena and Rome. For example, the Bolognese chronicler, the *Anonymous Bianchina*, wrote in 1496 that 'this disease affected both women and men, and the majority caught it through coitus' (Corradi, 1884, 344). The Genoese chronicler, Agostino Giustiniano, the Dominican Bishop of Nebio, recorded that the Mal Francese 'began in the genital members for both men and women' (Corradi, 1884, 343).

Increased observation and experience of the Great Pox led chroniclers to understand better its nature and methods of transmission. Greater onus was now placed on women as the transmitters. Fileno delle Tuatte of Bologna declared that 'women have it in their nature', as did Portoveneri of Pisa: 'it's caught by frequenting women who have these diseases' (Corradi, 1884, 346; Portoveneri, 1845 ed., 338: 1502). Similarly, Francesco Murlati wrote: 'The beginning of this disease was detected from the woman's vulva, for a man who had intercourse with a woman suffering from that disease first felt an itch on the rod' (Corradi, 1884, 361). Delle Tuatte emphasised that prostitutes and courtesans were most likely to pass on the sickness, which he remarked led to their ejection from Bologna and Ferrara (Corradi, 1884, 346). In other places such as in London in 1506, brothels were closed briefly. It is difficult to say whether these measures were more generally linked to the threat of the Pox or whether they were part of broader policies against beggars and the poor at times of crisis (Pelling, 1986, 87; Quétel, 1990, 66–7; Schleiner, 1993; Fabricius, 1994, 61–2; Siena, 1998, 559). In any event, they were only temporary expedients, since it was seen as better to control prostitutes than to leave them unregulated, and some cities regarded prostitutes as preferable to sodomy (Hewlett, 2005, 256; Cohn, 2018, 120–1).

The theme of sexual transmission remained common to the second and third generations of Italian chroniclers. Cirillo Bernardino (1500–75), protonotary and papal secretary, who finished writing his *Annali* of Aquila in 1540, declared that the French 'infected the women of the region with the contagion, and these infected women infected those with whom they came into contact' (Corradi, 1884, 365). Writing in the late 1530s, Guicciardini agreed, but also described changes in the nature of the disease; initially it 'killed many people of both sexes and of all ages, and many became very deformed, rendering them useless and subject to continuous torments. The majority of those who got better, returned after a short time to the same miserable state'. He also recorded that the disease was not static (Guicciardini, 1971 ed., 233):

> 'But after the course of many years, it became much less virulent, either as a result of the influence of the stars or because long experience had led to learning the right remedies to treat it. The disease became much less malignant, and also because it transformed itself in different types distinct from the initial one.'

In acknowledging the expertise of astrologers and medical practitioners, Guicciardini recognises that diseases, like humans, have life cycles, which cause them to grow stronger and to weaken. He then dismisses those who claimed that they had contracted it as one might catch influenza through the air: 'This calamity is certainly one which men of our time might justly complain about, if they caught it through no fault of their own: but all those who have diligently observed the nature of this illness agree that never, or very rarely, can anyone catch it except by contagion during coitus' (Guicciardini, 1971 ed., 234).

1.5 Conclusion

It has been argued that Italian chroniclers reflected more generally how contemporaries understood and reacted to what they saw as a 'new disease which arrived in Italy in these times' from the New World (Piero di Marco Parenti in: Corradi, 1884, 342). Initially across Europe a range of explanations was provided about its origins from the Moriscoes to prostitutes to more general factors, such as God's punishment for individual and society's sins, and astrological influence. However, in Italy chroniclers, unlike early medical writers, rarely cited planetary conjunction as a contributory cause for the epidemic of Mal Francese. This was in contrast to initial explanations for the Black Death, which was seen as God's punishment for the sins of mankind. But the two epidemics had significant differences. Plague killed indiscriminately large numbers of people within a few days, and the poor were blamed for fomenting and spreading the disease. For the Great Pox, which typically led to years of very painful sickness, commentators came to make connections between contracting the disease and physical contact and the blaming of women in particular as the main vehicles of contagion (Henderson, 2013). While Section 4 examines how this theme was developed in popular literature by linking disease, prostitution and immorality, the next section shows how a more morally neutral stance was adopted in the writings of many medical practitioners.

2 Pox and Medicine: Theory and Practice

2.1 Introduction

The eighteenth watercolour of the Perugian album (Figure 3) shows a young man sitting patiently on a stool, while a surgeon opens and cleanses an ulcer on his right arm; the tourniquet suggests that he may also have been bled. Despite his rather blank expression, the patient is clearly in a distressed state with red spots visible on his chest and on his legs and feet, while his left arm is in a sling; his legs are bandaged, probably covering ulcers treated with a mercury ointment. His head is covered loosely with another bandage, which may indicate he is suffering from further lesions or already losing hair, another symptom of the Great Pox.

Surgeons were central to treating the Pox, since many symptoms were external, though physicians were heavily invested in establishing its exact nature and recommending treatments. Chroniclers noted that the disease was unknown to doctors, and the emergence of a disease not described in the medical canon could

Figure 3 Surgeon treating a Pox patient (late sixteenth century),
(BCAP, MS G61, c. 50r)

potentially cast doubt on the whole edifice on which Renaissance medicine was based. This led to public debates in the 1490s concerning the nature of the French Disease, at the Ferrarese court, the University of Bologna, and later the University of Leipzig. Initially there were attempts to claim that it corresponded to diseases described by classical physicians, Galen (elephantiasis) and Hippocrates ('diseases of the summer'), but ultimately its novelty was recognised. Physicians then took ownership of it by Latinising the popular term to Morbus Gallicus, a first step in inspiring confidence in their ability to provide efficacious treatment (AHF, ch. 4, cf. Carmichael, 1990; Ciccarella, 2018–19, 1.3).

This section will begin by examining contemporary medical understanding of the Great Pox by comparing a selection of treatises by physicians and surgeons across the sixteenth century. The first is Antonio Benivieni, the Florentine physician to the Medici family, whose casebook *De Abditis Nollibus* was published posthumously in 1507. He reveals how a practising physician understood the nature of the disease within less than a decade of its first outbreak. The second and third physicians, Niccolò Massa (1485–1569) and Girolamo Fracastoro (c. 1478–1553), were from the following generation when the disease had begun to evolve. A briefer consideration will be given to the treatises of two surgeons, Giovanni Andrea della Croce (1583) and Leonardo Fioravanti (1561).

The writings of these five practitioners reflect how ideas of physicians and surgeons about the nature of the disease evolved over the sixteenth century. This will provide the background for discussion of the treatment of a range of practitioners both in private practice and within specialised Incurabili hospitals. But first, in order to understand the medical concepts of these authors, it is necessary to provide a brief outline of contemporary Galenic theory. Galenism, named after Galen of Pergamon in Asia, who flourished in the second century CE under the Roman Empire, informed university medical education and thus the practice of physicians and surgeons, and the basic ideas were shared by practitioners of empirical and domestic medicine. Galenic theory held that the human body was made up of four humours: blood, phlegm, choler, equivalent to red or yellow bile, and melancholy (black bile), and each was viewed as equivalent to four actual bodily fluids. Having said this, almost all internal illnesses were regarded as due to the complexional imbalance of an individual's humours according to their four main qualities: hot, cold, dry or moist. Furthermore, much of the explanation for the causes of the Great Pox was due to the influence of corrupt and potentially contagious matter, which derived from outside the body and led to the corruption of humours and putrefaction (Siraisi, 1990, 104–6; Wear, 2000). Initially, while some of the early medical writers in the 1490s, such as the Spanish doctors Per Pintor and Gaspar Torrella, who worked at the papal court in Rome, also alluded to divine and astrological primary causes of the epidemic, in time these ideas became less central (AHF, 110–111, 120–121; Cohn, 2018, ch. 5).

Treatment began with diagnosis; physicians examined excreta (and urine in particular), and took the pulse (Nutton, 2004, ch. 16). The aim was to re-establish the proper balance of health through the administration of simple and compound medicine, linked to an individual's complexional make-up. Doctors recommended internal interventions from purging and balancing humours through the administration of pills and electuaries to rid the body of the putrefaction associated with the disease. Surgeons undertook external treat-ment, including letting blood to purge the body of corruption, applying oint-ments and cauterisation to treat swellings, sores and lesions, and ultimately surgery for the removal of damaged or diseased limbs.

2.2 Physicians and Mal Francese

Benivieni began by describing the pustules, ulcers and pains in the joints mentioned by chroniclers, but was more specific in distinguishing different types and their effects (Benivieni, 1954 ed., 13). The first pustules he observed began near or on the genitals; as they spread they corroded the flesh and gave off a fetid and foul discharge, as did both pimples and larger pustules. When the scales associated with pustules fell off, they led to scarring and bleeding. This is reflected in the second Perugian watercolour (Figure 4), showing a fashionably dressed young man in doublet, ruff and hose with a hat decorated with two large

Figure 4 Young man with diseased genitals (late sixteenth century),
(BCAP, MS G61, c. 12r)

feathers. He is obviously in some pain since in addition to a red rash on his neck and upper nose, his hands around his genitals hold his penis, with red streaks suggesting a stream of blood.

Benivieni then went on to describe the symptoms and the causes of the disease (Benivieni, 1954 ed., 13):

> In my opinion the substance of these pustules varies as do the kinds of pustules. For sometimes a sharp humour, erosive and mixed with blood, predominates. Sometimes the thicker is separated from the thinner part of the fluid and turns to black bile. Sometimes too the black bile itself rises up and without separating itself from the sharper humour, pierces and eats away the flesh. Dried up discharges, inclining to resemble black bile in composition, act similarly.

Symptoms, ranging from different sizes and types of pustules to scales of skin to a corrosive discharge were interpreted as being caused by the corruption of the humour of black bile. Thus, for Benvieni black bile took on a pathological character and became a physical agent, which corroded the flesh, as did the dried discharges. Having determined the diagnosis, Benivieni emphasised that a trained physician must provide treatment, warning against unskilled practitioners, whose use of certain ointments had led to patients developing into an incurable state and dying prematurely. Instead, Benivieni stresses the need to rid the body of the corrupt humours, especially black bile, either through blood-letting, leeches or cupping glasses, followed by taking medicines to loosen the bowels and hence 'to draw off the humour you seek to evacuate ... since the moisture cannot be drawn off by one evacuation only, it will be necessary to repeat the dose frequently' (Benivieni, 19).

Massa developed the explanation further in his *Book of the French Disease*, published in Latin in 1524, twenty-two years after Benivieni's death (Massa, 1566, 14: Italian ed.). Based on a wealth of clinical knowledge of patients with Mal Francese and dissections of their bodies, Massa interpreted the cause of the disease as the liver becoming frigid and dry, reflecting its complexional quality. This led corrupt humours to spread through the body via a patient's veins, and in turn to pustules breaking out all over the skin. Following Galen and the Arabic physician Avicenna, Massa argued that while it was rare a single humour caused disease, nevertheless one humour was often dominant, as we have seen in the case of black bile, and it caused specific symptoms on the surface of the body (Massa, 1566, 14: Italian ed.):

> Therefore, when the matter mixed in the pustules is bloody, they appear red and raised, large, swollen and humble; if there is a mixture of choler the pustules are ruddy, without being greatly swollen and with dryness; if they appear with the mixture of melancholic humour, the pustules are bad, livid and shaped like oyster shells. (*ostracose*)

Benefitting from more experience of the disease, Massa is more specific than Benivieni in his differentiation between different types of pustules, likening some to an oyster shell. The third physician, Fracastoro, gradually evolved his ideas about the Great Pox from the 1520s. His first publication on the subject was the Latin poem, *Syphilis or the French Disease* (1530), followed by a short unpublished treatise of 1533, though his ideas were most developed in a substantial section of his 1546 Latin treatise, *On Contagion* (*De contagione*). If it had a much less wide circulation than treatises written in the vernacular, he provides a very useful and detailed guide to contemporary ideas of the nature of the disease (Pellegrini, 1939; Peruzzi, 1997; Henderson, 2006; Ciccarella, 2018–19, 1.5).

Fracastoro placed Mal Francese within a wider context than Benivieni or Massa. He saw it as part of a family of contagious diseases, which attacked the exterior rather than the interior parts of the body (Fracastoro, 1930 ed., 149):

> [I]t is clear that the principles of this contagion were analogous with thick, foul phlegm. For if we consider the pustules which appeared in this malady, the gummata, and the pains in the muscles, we shall see everywhere only mucus and foulness, and finally viscous, mucilaginous, thick phlegm.

In contrast to earlier authors, Fracastoro saw the causative agent as deriving from outside the body, and in particular from putrefaction of the air, mirroring explanations provided in many plague tracts from the time of the Black Death onwards. For Fracastoro, contagion and putrefaction were spread by 'seeds of disease', which, through their viscous quality, could attach themselves to clothes and be absorbed through breath and the pores: 'We must therefore suppose that ... there had stolen into the air a certain foul putrefaction which later proved to be analogous with the thick, foul phlegm in our bodies' (Fracastoro, 1930 ed., 149; Nutton, 1983).

Fracastoro shared the observation of other writers, such as Massa and Guicciardini, that the disease had evolved over time. He distinguished between the first thirty years from its initial appearance in 1494, from the following twenty years. In this initial phase, the major symptoms lay dormant for up to four months, but the individual became melancholic, lacking in energy and had a pallid complexion (Fracastoro, 1930 ed., 139). When the symptoms broke out, there was a preponderance of pustules with fewer of the larger gummata Benivieni had observed. Fracastoro regarded the later phase as characterised by drier pustules, more acute pains, and, from about 1540, loss of hair and teeth (Fracastoro, 1930 ed., 141). In the following decade, Pietro Rostinio, in his Italian treatise (1556) based on Musa Brasavola's Latin treatise (1553), confirmed that the disease had changed since the 1490s with the emergence of three different types, reflecting its decline (Rostinio, 1565 ed., 2–4; McGough, 2011, 65–6).

Fracastoro also observed that the main method of transmission had changed: 'since the original disposing cause which had been in the air had now ceased to exist, the disease had no other means of propagating itself than by contagion from one person to another' (Fracastoro, 1930 ed., 156–7). This occurred 'only when two bodies in close contact with one another became extremely heated. Now this happened in sexual intercourse especially, and it was by this means that the great majority of persons were infected' (Fracastoro, 1930 ed., 135). The transition to direct physical contact as the main cause of infection suggested to Fracastoro that the disease would ultimately disappear, for it was now in its old age and, like the humours of the elderly, 'the substance becomes colder and colder every day' (Fracastoro, 1930 ed., 157).

This discussion of the nature of the disease has shown that for contemporaries the essence of Mal Francese was phlegm, putrefaction and corruption of the humours, and the main aim of treatment was their elimination through the use of internal and external medicines. Sweating was an important evacuative method, and among the most popular sudorific was China root imported from South America, which had an important drying quality, essential when dealing with phlegm caused by putrefaction (Quétel, 1990, 63; Winterbottom, 2015). The use of heat is reflected in Figure 1; a male patient with bare feet is seated on a stool in front of a fire and wears a turban to avoid heat loss and hide loss of hair.

Fear of the dangerous effects of traditional, more drastic treatments involving mercury sublimates, often administered by surgeons and empirics, led Fracastoro and other contemporaries to recommend what was to become a specific against the French Disease, Guaiac wood. First mentioned in 1516, this hard and resinous wood was imported from the West Indies (Hispaniola). Its virtues were described by Fracastoro in his poem *Syphilis* (1984 ed., 87–9):

> The land [Hispaniola] is fertile in gold, but made far richer by one tree – they call this in the sounds of their native speech Guaiacum …the wood is almost like hard iron … That foreign race adores this tree and is very eager in its efforts to rear it …. Nor is anything more sacred to them or of more important use; for all hope lies in it against this plague, which the heavens have there made eternal.

Holy Wood was very expensive since it was imported from 'the Indies' and could only be afforded by the affluent and be administered by a physician (Shaw and Welch, 2011, 298–9). Poorer patients could gain access to this miraculous drug through Incurabili hospitals, as they did in other European cities, such as the Pox hospitals of Augsburg and London (AHF, ch. 8; Siena, 2005, 209; Stein, 2009, 147–52). When Holy Wood and physicians' treatment failed, private patients resorted to surgeons and empirics who treated symptoms on the visible body parts, especially the face, torso and limbs, as reflected in the Perugian watercolours.

2.3 Surgeons

Surgeons rarely wrote entire treatises on the French Disease, discussing it within more general works, such as in Giovanni Della Croce's *Cirurgia universale* (De Ferrari, 1988; Latin ed.: 1573; Italian ed.: 1583). The section in Book 5 on Mal Francese consists of a dialogue between a father and son about the nature of the disease and available treatments. The discussion is heavily dependent on the medical classics and echoes Massa's discussion: 'The French Disease is a certain type of poison, which does not travel immediately to the heart, but because of its properties goes to the liver, and corrupts it together with the blood, from whence various affections arise' (Della Croce, 1583, c. 33 r).[5] Della Croce mentions symptoms familiar from other contemporary descriptions, such as genital buboes, and burning sensation during urinating, as well as common treatments to remove the cause of the disease through evacuation and purging by administering Holy Wood, sarsaparilla and China root. He does not rule out the application of mercury sublimates by a surgeon, who is an expert in using potentially dangerous treatments for; he argues that sometimes it is better to use a violent remedy than let a patient die (Della Croce, 1583, c. 53 r).

Many of these treatments, even when recommended by physicians, were the province of a surgeon. Della Croce has separate chapters on how to deal with the different types and sizes of pustules. In Chapter VII, he recommended unguents to wash and treat ulcers or *brosole* on the genital area (Della Croce, 1583, c. 44 r). He also discusses the opening and draining of the larger swellings, known as 'buboes, tumours and gummata', which appear after the genital ulcers as the disease develops. These symptoms reflect the changes in the nature of disease with larger gummata and buboes in the groins, also one of the classic features of plague, from which he died in 1575.

Symptoms of genital disease are clearly represented in two of the initial watercolours in the Perugian album (Figures 5–6). The first shows a well-dressed young man about town, with ruff, doublet, trunk hose, cloak and sword, who supports his penis in his right hand from which flows a stream of black urine, which Fracastoro listed as one of the symptoms of Mal Francese, while his left arm is flung out as in pain. In the second watercolour he holds his penis to facilitate the treatment of a surgeon, who is probing a deep ulcerated sore on his inner thigh, reflecting Della Croce's treatment to open and drain the larger gummata. Both images show the man with red marks on his face, and the

---

[5] 'Il Mal Francese è un certo veleno, il quale non corre immediatamente al cuore, ma per sua proprietade va al fegato, e lo corrompe insieme col sangue, onde poi varii affettine nascono ... Overo dire che il Mal Francese è ... una certa cattiva dispositione de' membri nutritivi nel fegato ... dalla quale si generano varii humori velenosi e di mala natura ... '.

Figure 5 Young nobleman with black urine (late sixteenth century),
(BCAP, MS G61, c.7r)

first shows brighter red marks over his left eye, nose and mouth, and a red rash on his lower face and neck.

When none of these treatments worked, the surgeon resorted to cauterisation of ulcers and of festering wounds, as in the case of a young man in Figure 7. A military surgeon applies a red-hot cautery iron to the right-hand sole foot of a young man, dressed in doublet and shirt, who is yelling in agony. A small brazier fire and bellows indicate the source of the heat. The patient is clearly in a more advanced stage of his disease. The legs and feet are covered with red lesions, as is his left hand, and whether the symptoms shown here were the gummata of Mal Francese or battle wounds as a result of explosion of firearms, the principle of treatment remained the same.

Della Croce was part of the medical establishment, and he contrasts the potentially harmful effects of treatment provided by empirics with the beneficial effects of formal medicine based on 'the three famous instruments: Diet, Pharmacy and Surgery' (Della Croce, 1583, c. 41 r). Leonardo Fioravanti, by

Figure 6 Surgeon treating ulcerated sore on right thigh (late sixteenth century), (BCAP, MS G61, c. 9r)

contrast, challenges this learned tradition in fascinating ways. Trained as a surgeon, he argued that the effectiveness of treatments should be grounded in experience rather than theory, rejecting so-called scientific medicine based on the ancient Greek and Roman tradition (Eamon, 1998, 7–16). The Great Pox provided Fioravanti with the perfect vehicle for advancing his claims and at first this led to personal success. In Palermo he cured a Spanish noble and was subsequently appointed to direct the Incurabili hospital, followed by the grant of a licence to administer guaiacum by the Roman College of Physicians. However, his irascible character and personal attacks on members of the medical establishment led him to being banned from practising in both Rome and Venice.

Many of Fioravanti's ideas and recommended treatments, including for Mal Francese, were described in his *Capricci medicinali* (1561), which reached

Figure 7 Military surgeon cauterising Pox ulcers (late sixteenth century),
(BCAP, MS G61, c. 47r)

a wide readership, going through fifteen editions in Italian, and was translated
into French and German (Eamon, 1998, 9). His notion of the nature and causes
of Mal Francese was not new; for example, he explained the malady was caused
by corrupt and putrid humours linked to the malfunction of the liver, and nor
was his description of pains, boils, pustules, ulcers and smell (Fioravanti, 1561,
23–6, 189–90). More controversial was his discussion of the impact of the
disease on both internal and external body parts, eschewing the traditional
distinction of the medical profession. He also criticised physicians' over-
reliance on diet and 'weak' medicines as ineffective, instead advocating heroic
treatments based on strong emetics and purgatives, including 'evacuating the
stomach from a certain viscous putrefaction, which is generated by the corruption of the disease' (Fioravanti, 1561, 189). Pills of hellebore, senna and crocus
were administered to the patient to create a great vomit, followed by the
administration of mercury. The principles underlying Fioravanti's treatment of
Mal Francese differed little from those of physicians; it was his cantankerous

character and above all the assumption that he could administer internal medicines that aroused opposition. Fioravanti claimed his success was based on his experience in treatment. However, historians of Mal Francese in Italy have tended to concentrate on treatises than practice, so we shall examine briefly the treatment provided by physicians and surgeons within Incurabili hospitals, and then the role of empirics and non-licensed practitioners.

2.4 Incurabili Hospitals and the Poor

Incurabili hospitals were founded in the sixteenth century in many cities across Italy from Venice to Palermo, specifically in response to the problems caused for poorer members of society by the explosion of Mal Francese. One of the significant features of these new institutions was their size, building on the tradition of large-scale Italian medical hospitals. One particularly well-documented example was San Giacomo in Rome, which developed from an existing hospital for the poor sick to the south of Piazza del Popolo, with the façade of the church fronting onto Via del Corso. There were three main periods of expansion, the first under Leo X (1519–26), when the original male ward was enlarged, as was the female ward in the following two decades. The most significant development, under the patronage of Cardinal Antonio Maria Salviati, led to building a new male ward and a new elliptical-shaped church behind the façade designed by Carlo Maderno and completed by Francesco da Volterra; the façade can be seen in Giovan Battista Falda's view of 1676 (Figure 8). We can see the scale of the male ward, the Corsia Salviati (now called Corsia Genga) from an early twentieth-century photograph when the hospital was still in use (Figure 9). When built it was 100 metres in length, 10 metres wide and had 263 beds over two floors. By 1581, San Giacomo treated annually some 2,200 male and female patients in two vast wards, even as it turned away many more seeking admission (De Angelis, 1955, 7, 9–14, AHF, ch. 8).

San Giacomo, as at the other Italian Incurabili, employed a large administrative and nursing staff, who provided the food and medicines to enable the physicians and surgeons to put into operation the forty-day regime of treatment of Holy Wood. Preparations were made well before the doors were opened. Carpenters were employed to make further beds to be placed between the existing rows, as well as to seal the windows to keep in the warm air from the fires lit to heat the ward. Sweating in a well-heated ward and purging were an essential part of treatment along with a light diet and the administration of medicines prepared in the apothecary's shop. These included aloe pills, hellebore, with strong, simple medicines, such as China root, to evacuate putrefied humours and morbid matter. Large quantities of Guaiacum were prepared in

Figure 8 Giovan Battista Falda, *Church and hospital of San Giacomo degli Incurabili*, Via del Corso, Rome (1676). (Creative Commons Attribution-ShareAlike 3.0 license)

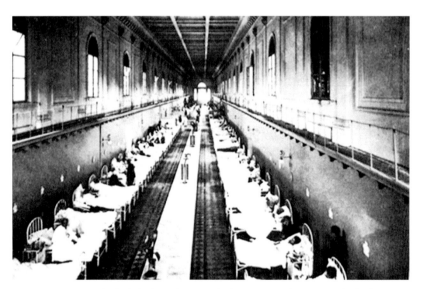

Figure 9 Corsia Salviati, early twentieth-century view, Hospital of San Giacomo degli Incurabili (Photo: Marco Ciaramella: Creative Commons Attribution-Share Alike 4.0 International license)

three different stages, each with a different but related purpose. The wood, first cut up into small pieces and soaked in water, was boiled until reduced to half its original volume. The foam produced was dried and used as a drying powder on sores; a concentrated solution was drunk regularly; and a weaker solution, obtained by re-boiling the wood, was drunk during meals. While this treatment followed the recommendations of the medical treatises examined above, none of the doctors give a hint of what the sensory experience of the administration of a full course of Guaiacum would have been like. Although large and airy, the wards would have been insufferably hot, particularly in the summer months, and full of the smells associated with evacuation of bodily liquids and the cries of severely sick men and women (Henderson, 2006).

2.5 Empirics

While Incurabili hospitals did treat the poorer members of society, few had access to their services if they lived in remote areas. Instead, they could turn to empirics, whose petitions to medical colleges for licences provide evidence of their treatment of Mal Francese. Protectionism, whether protecting the role of official practitioners from the incursion of unlicensed interlopers or patients from possible harm, remained a feature of medical colleges across Europe (Pomata, 1998; Pelling, 2003; Gentilcore, 2005). Many of their existing archives contain references to the French Disease, especially as it proved to be such a challenge to the medical profession. Some examples were published by Alfonso Corradi from the Roman College, which received petitions from practitioners claiming to specialise in the Pox, including twelve from 1559 to 1566. Seven petitioners were surgeons, including one, Dominus Jacobo Longo, from Messina, who, 'notwithstanding his clerical status', was permitted to treat Mal Francese, as well as 'pains and other infirmities', using Holy Wood (Corradi, 1884, 350–2). A surgeon from Padua, called Bernardo Vittorio, provided a detailed description of his skills in 1559 (Corradi, 1884, 352–3):

> to treat bodies through surgery, and also in more serious cases of ulcers and wounds and abscesses, and extracting the stone from the bladder, scrubbing off a consolidating wound, operating on occlusions, extracting pus and the like, and treating the French Disease, and using a certain artificial or magisterial Balzarine oil for nerve wounds and punctures and tears and incisions and other cold diseases, and also healing remedies for the teeth.

This long list of specialities secured the College's approval, for Vittorio was given a licence in perpetuity to practise many of a surgeon's normal duties, including the use of his special Balzarine oil. Other surgeons were granted licences for more specific activities, as with Benedetto di Girolamo from Parma, who specialised in venereal afflictions among other skin diseases, 'to be able to treat and draw out [infections of] the skin and flesh of the rod, and the French disease and scrofula and other things pertaining to surgery' (Corradi, 1884, 354). For some practitioners, especially those who were not trained surgeons, the College restricted the medicines they could use, including mercurial ointments.

The archive of the College of Physicians of Florence, which covered grand ducal Tuscany, also contains even more petitions for licences to treat the French Disease, as well as pleas from patients asking the College to permit certain treatments, and prosecutions of practitioners discovered using prohibited methods and medicines.[6] Seven of the ten cases associated with the French Disease between September 1560 and March 1564 were petitions from medical practitioners. Four were registered as surgeons, but used treatments prohibited by the College. Two used heat from a dry stove, 'stufa secca', to sweat out the disease. Maestro Benedetto Petrini was forbidden to employ this treatment because it was regarded as 'too audacious'; probably it involved the use of mercury sublimate, but he was still allowed to continue with weaker treatments. In his petition, Petrini countered that he would like to resume his previous practice, but with the advice of a physician, thus cleverly bowing to the authority of the medical profession.[7]

Two petitions in 1562 from patients pleaded that a Castelfiorentino surgeon be allowed to treat their Mal Francese. Both were evidently suffering from the extreme symptoms, with Bernardo di Simone Gazzetti declaring that 'it prevents him from speaking, as he attests, and devours his face'.[8]

His state is shown in the eleventh Perugian watercolour of a man reduced to begging in the final stages of his illness (Figure 10). He is shown with torn clothes, wild hair, corroded nose and a body covered with red sores and the more serious black pustules.

Evidently, the Castelfiorentino surgeon had gained a reputation for success, since Bernardo declared that he 'relies on the practices which he had seen him undertake'.[9] The problem was that the surgeon's licence had been revoked because he had used 'violent stoves for the French Disease, without the physician's orders'.[10] In the event the College permitted the surgeon to use these treatments, though only for these patients and only if both took responsibility for the effects: 'If he wants him to kill him, let him do it' and 'if he wants to choke himself, let it be restricted to him.'[11]

---

[6] Archivio di Stato di Firenze (ASF), Ospedale di Santa Maria Nuova (SMN), 192–193.

[7] ASF, SMN 193, no. 170, 21.2.1561/2; 305, 14.7.1563.

[8] ASF, SMN 193, no. 241: 'l'impedisce il favellare come produce fede et li divora il viso'.

[9] ASF, SMN 193, no. 241: 'confida nelle sperienzie che dice haverli viste fare'.

[10] ASF, SMN 193, no. 220: 'le stufe violenti per il malfranzese, senza l'ordinatione del fisico', and 'medicare con stufe, untioni et profumi'.

[11] ASF, SMN 193, no. 241: 'Se egli vuole che l'ammazzi faccia lui' and 'se vuoli stroppiarsi sia ristretto in lui'.

Figure 10 Beggar with diseased body and face (late sixteenth century),
(BCAP, MS G61, c. 31r)

Patients were not the only people to respect the expertise of a wide range of practitioners to treat the disease. In August 1561, the physician Maestro Cristiano Pagni petitioned the grand duke on behalf of Pellegrino da Casabasciana of the Lucchese *contado*, who wished 'to treat Mal Franzese, gouts and other incurable conditions' in the Tuscan state, especially in the Valdinievole. Pagni asked the College to relax its own regulations and allow Pellegrino to practise without being obliged to be examined. Unsurprisingly, the College replied that '[t]he law prohibits anyone to offer medical treatment, who has not been approved by this office'.[12] Maestro Cristiano's interest in this matter had been provoked by the claim that Pellegrino had cured a patient with Mal Francese, and had offered to cure within fifteen days somebody from Pescia, who had gout and could only walk with the help of crutches (*croccie*). Cristiano petitioned that Pellegrino should be allowed to continue with his treatment, so that he could observe how it worked and that he himself could experiment with the 'secret of the doctor'. The grand duke had given his permission for this to go ahead, so the College had to agree, even though 'we don't believe in it'! It stipulated, however, that Maestro Cristiano should supervise the *cura* and that Pellegrino could only undertake this treatment; for anything else he would need to be examined by the College.

This case involves a series of participants: Pellegrino, who was described as 'a doctor'; the petitioning physician Maestro Cristiano; the grand duke, who

---

[12] SMN 193, 126: 30.8.1561.

was able to override the College's privileges; and the College, which was forced to make an exception. The College also maintained its authority, limiting Cristiano's permission to practise without proper authorisation, and placed this 'experiment' under the supervision of the physician. It also involved the local secular authority, stipulating that the Vicar, the local administrative representative of the Florentine government, should carefully observe its success.

A broadly similar story emerges from the cases of three women who treated Mal Francese. Women were excluded from the privileged circle of those who could belong to the medical guild – physicians, surgeons and apothecaries – but, nonetheless, played a valuable role as healers within society. The College had granted licences to each of these women at some stage in their careers, but these licences were limited and when the women did not follow the restrictions, they incurred the College's displeasure. Monna Agnola di Agnolo da Cannaia had come to the College's notice three times over a two-year period from September 1560.[13] She declared that she had worked for many years treating those with Mal Francese, using 'certain stoves' to make the patient sweat. Monna Agnola also specialised in treating poor women with the disease and that they preferred her over male practitioners. Finally, while admitting that she had given medicine through the mouth, she claimed this was only as an assistant to a physician. It was during the questioning of Monna Agnola that they discovered that she had used 'cinnabar and other violent things, inimical to nature'.[14] The College had heard that Monna Agnola's treatment had led to deaths, and people becoming crippled. A year later she returned to ask for the reversal of her sentence, supported by evidence from a series of patients whom she had cured.[15] Clearly, the College was not impressed since it reiterated its decision, declaring that treatment using the stoves was too violent, especially leaving them in the hands of a woman without knowledge of medicines.[16] In October 1562, Monna Agnola managed to get the decision reversed, following the intervention of the grand duke, who employed her husband as a coachman. However, the College stipulated that she was only allowed to practise on those patients whom physicians 'themselves did not want to lay on their hand, and especially poor people'.[17]

The second woman was Monna Lena detta la Biancha, who described herself as a 'very poor widow, with six little nephews, four female and two male'.[18]

---

[13] SMN 63: 24.9.1560.

[14] SMN 192, 142: 'cinabri et simili cose violente, et nimiche alla natura'.

[15] SMN 142: 10.12.1561.

[16] SMN 193, no. 142: 'quelle stufe fussero troppo violente a lasciarle in mano di una donna senza ragione di medicamenti'.

[17] SMN 224: 16.10.62: 'loro stessi non volessero metter la mano, et maxime i poveri persone'.

[18] SMN 195, no. 1: 'poverissima vedova, con sei nipoti, 4 femine et dua maschi'.

She petitioned for a reversal of the decision prohibiting her from her practice, even though she had followed their stipulations 'not to give anything by mouth and not to use arsenic, neither solimate nor mercury, and always to take advice from other doctors and to use all modesty and ensure that no one will be able to complain about her'.[19] Evidently, the petition carried some weight as it was presented by Maestro Tommaso de' Medici on behalf of the grand duchess, who had said she wanted Monna Lena to be allowed to continue to practise, as long as she abided by the restrictions listed in the petition. These were to be enforced by the duchess's own doctor, the surgeon Maestro Lorenzo Venturini, or, failing him, the physician Maestro Pietro da Perugia. With the grand duchess's support, everything should have gone smoothly for Monna Lena. However, the College discovered that Monna Lena had used the hot stove treatment on a certain prostitute with Mal Francese, without the permission of either Maestro Lorenzo or Maestro Pietro. The College fined her twenty-five *scudi*, which she then petitioned to be rescinded since she could not afford it – it was equivalent to about 150 days' wages for an unskilled worker! – and had said that she was unable to obtain the license from the doctors, since one was sick and the other absent.

2.6 Conclusion

These cases reveal that while official treatment was supplied by physicians and surgeons, patients also resorted to empirics, especially as there was no guarantee that College members were more successful (Pelling, 2003). Empirics also had the advantage of charging much lower fees than the privileged cartel of College practitioners. In Italy, as elsewhere, this privileged cartel sought to control the medical marketplace, to defend their own privileges, earn revenues from fines and to guarantee quality. Colleges were part of a wider governmental structure, and direct appeals to higher authority in the shape of the ruler might lead to intervention. Even if this resulted in clemency and the reversal of an earlier decision, the College still forbade outsiders to go beyond the terms stipulated. The granting of licences to non-members, including empirics and women, suggests a slightly more flexible approach to treatment than reflected in official regulations or in the treatises of physicians and surgeons, though this flexibility varied across societies. The success of a practitioner depended on their reputation and consumer demand, but also on the constraints and costs imposed by medical guilds and Colleges. Patients themselves often had their

---

[19] SMN, 195.1: 17.6.1562: 'di non potere dare nulla per boccha et non adoperare arsenicho ne solimato ne ariento vivo, et sempre consigliarsi con altri medici et usare ogni modestia et farà in modo che nessuno non si potrà lamentare di lei'.

own ideas and relied on practitioners from a wide variety of backgrounds to provide them with treatment, as we shall see in the following section.

3 Pox and Patients

3.1 Introduction

Ser Tommaso di Silvestro, a canon of Orvieto cathedral, provides one of the first, most detailed accounts of the personal experience of Mal Francese. In 1497, he had contracted the disease, but then recovered. His description survives in his chronicle of Orvieto, which records numerous public natural disasters, including plague and famine (*Diario*, 69):

> There came to me certain pains, first in the knees on the feast-days of Christmas 1496, and then from January, I declined rapidly, and I took the treatment of five syrups and a course of pills. Finally, a while after taking the pills, I suffered from certain pains on the top of my left shoulder and in the kidneys and buttocks and this lasted until May.

A year later, on 26 April 1498, his symptoms returned with greater ferocity (*Diario*, 101):

> [O]n my return from the fair at Foligno, my rod began to pain me, and from then the sickness increased every day afterwards. From then until 8 June, I began to have the pains of the French Disease. And I felt a burning sensation all over my head with scabs that burned, and I felt pains in my right and left arms, all the way from the shoulder to the knuckle; it created such pain in my bones that I couldn't find rest. Then I had pain in my right knee, and then boils erupted all over the front and back of my torso, and then after the Feast of Corpus Christi, I was treated with medicines and blood-letting, and then ointments for the pains and boils, applied by a friar, Oliviere, who was staying at Benano. I remained six days continuously in bed, and at the end of the seventh, the Feastday of Saints Peter and Paul, the last day of June, he bathed me with a hot fomentation of wine and many herbs, including absinthe, mint, rosemary, garden sage and other herbs. And on Sunday I began to go out of the house, that is the first of July.
>
> Item, it left me with great pain in the mouth, which lasted thirty-six days, so I could barely eat baked bread; and the pain in the arm and sores went away after fourteen days. But there remained a great pain in my mouth and then, on 22 July, I suffered from a flux, which lasted two days, from which I nearly died. And then from the month of November the pains in my legs began to heal.

These passages give a vivid description of the symptoms of the French Disease within the first few years of the beginning of the epidemic. They coincide in broad terms with those discussed by medical writers, though without any allusion to theories of disease. Ser Tommaso was fortunate since he survived for another two decades, but he recorded the names of various compatriots, who died of the disease over the next few years. Ser Tommaso's discussion of his symptoms is unusually detailed, since it was based on personal experience. In his first attack, he suffered from pains, on his left shoulder, kidneys and buttocks. In the second episode pains spread to his arms and knee and mouth, and then to his genitalia, and scabs developed on his head and boils on his torso. The first round of treatment consisted of a five-syrup electuary and pills, and later he was prescribed blood-letting and a soothing ointment and a hot fomentation of herbs. Significantly, he chose to be treated by a friar rather than by a licensed practitioner, who did have medical knowledge and used herbal remedies, thus avoiding the more violent treatments involving mercury.

In common with many contemporaries during the early stages of this 'new disease', Ser Tommaso recorded his own sufferings as uncomfortable, but does not mention how it was contracted, even if he suffered from pain in his 'rod'. In the 1490s, there was no automatic assumption of a close link between the sickness and sexual transmission and the two prostitutes whom he recorded as dying in Perugia in these years allegedly perished from other diseases. His coyness in not mentioning how he had his illness may arise from a desire to maintain his reputation as a public figure and cathedral canon, but also reflects the theory of transmission widespread at this early stage of the epidemic, that the malady 'is passed on . . . through eating and through drinking and through sexual relations' (Friano degli Ubaldini: Corradi, 1884, 345).

The contemporary accounts by non-medical men examined in this section differ from the chroniclers and medical men examined in previous sections since they are based, either directly or indirectly, on personal experience of the French Disease. They range from the correspondence of the ruling Este family in Ferrara to burlesque poetry and plays and the autobiography of Benvenuto Cellini. Even if some accounts reflect literary tropes rather than based on direct experience, they nevertheless are based on contemporary lay knowledge of the disease. Interleaved with this discussion will be an analysis of the Perugian watercolours, which present a nuanced and vivid picture of the impact of the Pox on the human body, depicting a wide range of individuals of different ages. The album also traces the evolution of the disease through a series of images of a specific patient, whose decadence emerges from his increasingly ravaged appearance, shabby dress and final destitution.

Figure 11 is one of three watercolours of a young man dressed in a green-buttoned tunic, seated on a tree-stump, with one hand holding a hat or turban on his head, to hide his hair loss. His face is covered with marked red raised lesions, and the visible parts of his legs that are around the knee also have red ulcers, and the right leg is bandaged. Most importantly, the watercolours focus on the sufferings of the patient, unusual for medical illustrations in this period, where patients are normally shown with little expression, even when undergoing surgery.

Figure 11 Young man in a turban with red lesions (late sixteenth century), (BCAP, MS G61, c. 9r)

The album also includes two watercolours surrounded by a cornice showing two elegantly dressed young men (Plates 5–6). These images could illustrate Christian Berco's observation that a common contemporary perception in early modern Toledo was the close link between the disease with young male libertines, typified by Don Juan, who suffered well-deserved retribution for their sins (Berco, 2016, 23–9).

The association between Mal Francese and nobility is well-documented in the correspondence of members of the court of the Este Dukes of Ferrara. The jurist Bernardino Zambotti recorded its presence in the city in 1496: 'this disease seems to be incurable, since it is the disease of St Job; and it springs from men who do it with women in their vulva. As a result of it, most of these men die; they suffer from pains in bones and nerves, and very big pustules all over the body' (Zambotti, 267; AHF, 44). Among the first to be affected were members of the Este family from Isabella's husband, Francesco Gonzaga, Marquis of Mantua, to the three sons of Duke Ercole I d'Este, including his heir, Alfonso (AHF, 45–50; Bourne, 2008; James, 2020, 134–8, 169, 172–173). Ercole's concern, as we have seen, led to the promotion a public debate in Ferrara concerning the nature of the disease, helping to inform both Bernardino Zambotti's knowledge and that of his cousin Zaccharia, Ercole's favoured court physician (AHF, 46–48).

The correspondence of the Estense family and that between Duke Francesco Gonzaga and his wife Isabella reveals a striking absence of references to the term 'Mal Francese', though the disease was widespread in Ferrara. Moreover, there was a close resemblance between contemporary descriptions of its symptoms and treatment and those recorded in these letters. In Alfonso's letters to his father and his brother Ippolito, Cardinal of Milan, his language is evidently informed by the ducal physician, Ludovico Carri, who treated him, to which he added his own observations. In 1497, Alfonso reported that Carri had provided reassurance, that he was not very sick, and that his indisposition was due to having slept without bedcovers during a very hot night. However, by August 1499 he was seeking alternative remedies, asking Ercole to send oil of turpentine, cloves and storax to calm 'a certain pain … under my left knee that does not let me rest a moment all day and night' (AHF, 48–9, n. 64; Tosti, 1992, 56–60).

When Francesco's sickness returned after 1508, it is significant that the term Mal Francese is still avoided. Mario Equicola, humanist and courtier, sent a report in late April from Mantua to Ippolito in Milan describing Francesco's health in the following terms: 'Truly he does not feel very well. I do not know precisely what his ailment is, although I recall that in the beginning of March his genital member caused him great pain, and that later, in Gonzaga, he suffered from fevers. I am not sure what is afflicting him at present' (Bourne, 2008, 469–70; James, 2020, 134–5). Francesco, writing to Isabella a month earlier, recounted that, although he was afflicted by a severe fever and vomiting, the doctors had concluded that it was 'neither grave nor dangerous' (James, 2020, 134, n.1). The following April when on a military campaign against Venice, he wrote that his sleep was interrupted because he had a 'tremendous catarrh' and the following month he complained of appalling pains in his thighs (James, 2020, 138, n.15, 140 n.21, 141).

The repeated pains and sleeplessness with fevers and catarrh should have convinced Isabella that Francesco had Mal Francese, given that the symptoms were very well-known at the time, and her brothers suffered from the disease. In April 1508, Francesco came closer to admitting the cause of his condition in a message, which he asked to be forwarded to Louis XIII: 'tell the King it was probably caused by "love"' (James, 2020, 137 and n. 12). Although Francesco was careful not to mention the true cause of his condition to his wife, his symptoms coincide with contemporary descriptions, both of chroniclers and medical writers examined in Sections 1 and 2. It is telling of his attitude to his personal doctors to whom he had submitted himself for years to regimes of blood-letting and purging, that latterly he claimed greater relief from the ministrations of empirics. In 1514, he was treated by an empiric from Genoa, who gave him a 'certain drink and a certain water to bathe his infected eyes (*ochi offesi*)' (James, 2020, 169 n. 34). Later that year he had three days' treatment from a Franciscan, which he claimed had had miraculous effects, recalling Ser Tommaso's ministrations by a friar (James, 2020, 172).

Alfonso and Francesco's faith in their doctors lasted as long as they were successful and reassuring, and, in time, like Ser Tommaso, they turned to treatments they had heard were more efficacious and to practitioners outside the immediate court circle. These sources suggest that educated lay men and women had their own ideas about their illness and the most appropriate treatments.

3.2 Pox and Literary Autobiography

From personal letters, we turn to literary autobiography in renaissance Italy, and although many are relatively well-known, here they will be analysed to draw out their medical content, in particular authors' descriptions of Mal Francese and its symptoms. They are a very different type of source and have to be examined within the tradition of burlesque poetry (cf. Ciccarella, 2018–19, ch. 2). The authors were associated closely with some of the main literary academies in the sixteenth century, typified by a relaxed ribald atmosphere, reflected in their titles such as the Roman Accademia della Vigna, whose members were known as 'Vintners', the probably fictitious Accademia de' Balordi (hare-brained), and the Accademia degli Umidi (damp or humid), a satirical suggestion that its members had wet or humid humours leading to weak brains (Zanrè, 2005, 189, 192). The satirical nature of the genre leads one to be cautious when assessing the reliability of the poems and plays recited and performed in the literary academies. They were not transparent accounts, but rather literary topoi, and at times it is hard to work out how far they really did record personal experience. Even so, we shall argue that they do reflect general knowledge among the literate laity about the nature and symptoms of the French Disease.

Some ten years after Ser Tommaso's account, the Sienese poet and actor Niccolò Campani wrote *The Lament of Strascino* (*Lamento di quel tribolato di Strascino*), an allegedly autobiographical verse narrative account of his long eight-year battle with Mal Francese between 1503 and 1511. The work was divided into two parts. The first was written between 1509 and 1511 during the latter stages of the disease, and the second ten years later when he had recovered and was working at the papal court in Rome. Assuming he really did have the disease, it is doubtful that he truly recovered, since he died in 1523 at the relatively young age of forty-five, two years after his work had appeared in print (Alonge, 1974; Pieri, 2010; Ciccarella, 2018–19, 2.3; Gagné, forthcoming).

Ser Tommaso's chronicle and Campani's poem belong to different genres with very different conventions. While Ser Tommaso's is very evidently a personal account, albeit within a history of Orvieto, Campani's shares the form and function of the satirical poems and plays about the lives of prostitutes we shall examine in Section 4. Campani was well-known for his comedies and performances at Italian courts, including those of Mantua and Rome, where Mal Francese was rife.

The title of *The Lament* derives from a biblical model, most famously the Old Testament books of Jeremiah and Job. The relevance of the subtitle, 'patience and impatience', becomes clear when one recalls that the root of 'patience' (*patior*) means to suffer. The rich and powerful king of the land of Uz had a series of personal tragedies visited upon him, including skin disease, as a test of his faith. In the long run he was restored by God to his former state, but along the way he suffered the indignity of being wrongly accused by his wife and friends for being punished for his sins. The visual representation of Job is the subject of Section 5, for as patron saint of the Great Pox he was shown covered with spots and lying on a stinking dunghill, reflecting the association between corrupt air and disease.

The woodcut print on the title page of the 1564 edition of *The Lament* (Figure 12) shows the patient lying on a bed, with medical attendants replacing Job's wife and friends. Campani believed that the saint had more hope than him since his afflictions did not match the excruciating pains of Mal Francese (Campani, 1523, verses 50–3). The religious theme is emphasised by the devil flying above the patient, showering him with the disease, a diabolical reinterpretation of the Angel arriving with the palm of martyrdom. Behind the bed is an image of Christ, who had the power not just to inflict disease as punishment but also to take it away as the divine physician. These contradictory themes of 'patience and impatience' are at play throughout the poem. Campani's hope was that through patience and saying prayers and litanies, God would pardon him and the disease would pass. At times impatience took over and during his 'war of torments' he was moved to blasphemy, deciding it was better to invoke hell and demons. Finally, he reverted to his belief in divine punishment as the cause and believed that on recovery his tremendous suffering would purge him of all his sins (Campani, 1523, verses 10–21).

The image of the sick room strikingly underlines the themes of physical disease and medical treatment (cf. Gagné, forthcoming). The patient's whole body is covered with dark blotches representing the horrendous sores, pustules and ulcers generated by the Mal Francese. He is shown leaning back on his

Figure 12 Niccolò Campani, *The Lament of Strascino*, frontispiece
(Venice, 1564), (internet archive, Creative Commons,
Public Domain Mark 1.0)

pillow and gazing at the medical practitioner, who takes his pulse from the left arm. The physician carries around his waist a scroll, probably a urine chart, to aid diagnosis of the patient's condition, while the attendant holds a urine flask. The doctor and his attendants stand close to the bed, while behind them is an open window to cleanse the air of the smell produced by suppurating sores.

The poem traces the development of the author's illness, emphasising what life was like before he became sick, when he was 'cheerful and playful' as actor, poet and playwright at noble courts, while now 'my cheerfulness and sounds are converted into cries of pain', especially at night (Campani, 1523, verse 3). On the frontispiece of the *Lamento*, the patient expresses his emotions through his exclamation 'Alas the pains' ('Hoimè le doglie'), written on a scroll emerging from his mouth. As the poem progresses, his suffering worsened, moving from simply 'pain' to 'extreme pain', which makes him envy the dead and wish to die (Campani, 1523, verses 73–6). Dominique Brancher in her analysis of pox and pain in French literature at the time suggests that this genre represented a form of poetic therapy, in which the patient confronted and tamed the illness (Brancher, 2015, 55–6).

In addition to pain, Campani mentions that the disease remained hidden for four to six months before the familiar signs began to appear (Campani, 1523, verse 38). At that point, perhaps fearing the worst, but not yet suffering the full impact of the disease, he distances himself from his own experience and describes the torments suffered by those in the advanced stages (Campani, 1523, verse 42):

> Considering well all the ways
> That this disease transformed itself,
> Certain faces are scowling, distorted and ugly,
> Totally deformed from their natural appearance,
> Others with the skin eaten away to the bone,
> As in the tomb of a hospital
> Where one discerns the most valiant
> Without eyes, without nose and without teeth.

Here Campani emphasised the external signs most visible to an outside observer, but in his own case, he emphasises internal symptoms, as when he mentions the great heat caused by the disease, the pain in his mouth and the stink of disease on his breath. His throat was also affected, leaving him with a hoarse voice, and gave him no peace, being unable to eat or sleep, but only to cry aloud (Campani, 1523, verse 84). Campani does not go into detail concerning other more specific physical symptoms, particularly in relation to the impact on his limbs and parts of his body hidden from view, except to mention that he was afflicted by 'boils, sores, gummata, and pains' (Campani, 1523, verse 124). When he begins to recover, he is able to think in a more objective way, considering Mal Francese within a wider context, comparing his own disease with both podagra and gout. He concludes with an ironical comment that the major difference is that while gout is more selective, Mal Francese 'benefits' everybody (Campani, 1523, verse 132):

> The French Disease has more benefits
> Because it is pleasing to all people,
> Women, older and very young males,
> Religious, the rich and peasants.

Campani sought medical help to alleviate, if not cure, his symptoms. He recounts he wasted large sums on doctors' useless treatment, including sweating in a hot dry stove and mercurial ointments (Campani, 1523, verses 24, 27). Instead, he adopted his own remedies, despite the disagreement of medical professionals. He found temporary ways to 'comfort' or relieve the symptoms, including taking young garlic, modifying his diet and sitting in front of a roaring fire, drinking a lot of wine and mixing with lively companions (Campani, 1523, verses 28–32). All the latter expedients coincided with gentler preventative measures that were part of the six 'non-naturals', recommended by Galenic medicine to adjust the environmental conditions which affected a patient's body, such as heat and humidity, and their internal complexional balance which determined health. Ultimately, Campani did not lose faith in doctors, for he attributed his cure to Maestro Simone da Ronciglioni. He claims he had been cured by the application of mercury unguents to his sores and pustules. Such was his belief in Maestro Simone that he undertook seven courses of painful treatment, which he had earlier rejected, as well as 'Holy Wood', which he maintained helped prevent the disease from returning (Campani, 1523, verse 126).

He gives considerable detail about the development of the illness and treatment over the course of eight years. His account makes a telling comparison with Ser Tommaso di Silvestro's. With the benefit of twenty-five years, Campani knew what to expect in terms of the development of the sickness; Ser Tommaso instead had encountered an unknown disease without an established prognosis, which must have been bewildering. This development of knowledge was also true of the first medical writers examined in Section 2; for while Benivini had yet to develop a detailed description of the disease, by the time that Niccolò Massa was writing in the 1520s, a clearer idea had emerged of the symptoms similar to those recounted by Campani. However, neither Campani nor Ser Silvestro provides any idea of how they contracted it. This is in contrast to the putatively autobiographical pamphlet from the early 1520s, *The Seven Pains of the French Disease* (*Li sette dolori del Mal Francese*), possibly by the poet and actor Maestro Andrea Veneziano, whom we meet in Section 4, as author of *The Purgatory of the Courtesans*. He attributes the source of the disease to prostitutes, and ends with the admonition (*Sette dolori*, 1580 ed., verse 17):[20]

---

[20] 'Et hebbi spesso il mio libretto in mano
Che da putane tu starai lontano'.

> And I often have my little book in my hand
> So that thou shalt stay away from whores.

This pamphlet was also part of the tradition of burlesque poetry and was designed to be recited publicly in Rome in Piazza de' Sciarra, explaining the words above the image, 'a very enjoyable thing'. This type of pamphlet circulated widely and was printed cheaply in multiple copies; Campani's pamphlet went through fifty-seven editions before 1600 (Ciccarella, 2018–19, 307; Sampson, forthcoming).

The frontispiece of some editions of *The Seven Pains* (Venice, 1555) contains a woodcut showing a bearded male sufferer, whose nude body is covered with pustules and sores (Figure 13). He reclines on a bed, reflecting both Job on his dunghill and the figure shown on the frontispiece of Campani's *Lament*. The patient holds a fan in his left hand with which he attempts to assuage the heat of his pains and disperse the smell of decay. From the late sixteenth century, such images of Pox sufferers were reproduced on fans, thus acting as another medium through which knowledge of the disease was further popularised; it has been suggested they were also part of a broader movement emphasising the benefits of avoiding contagious diseases and adopting a healthy way of life (Strocchia and Kelly, 2022).

The theme of pain runs through this pamphlet. It outlines in detail the different stages of the disease, which first affected the brain to 'demonstrate its power and valour, and made lord of the fortress' (*Sette dolori*, 1580, verses 3–4). This 'cruel passion', the 'cruel and little mean pain', was felt all day and night in both the head and temples. The second phase of the disease moved from internal to external symptoms affecting the face (*Sette dolori*, 1580, verse 7):[21]

> This is a pain that pelts you, torments you,
> And makes you stand in shameful mockery:
> And you can then swear zealously,
> That thy face is clean of every hair.

The poor patient is teased about his appearance. He compares his hairless face to a frowning falcon, or a featherless starling or an ape, since there was not a hair left on his face, although he jokes that on the positive side, he will save money on barbers. On the negative side, he has to spend a lot on medicines, including oils and syrups or waters to bathe in, though none of this did anything to prevent

---

[21] 'Quest'è un duol che ti pela, ti tormenta,
  E ti fa star di vergogna schernito:
  E poterai giurar poi di buon zelo,
  Ch'l viso tuo è' netto d'ogni pelo'.

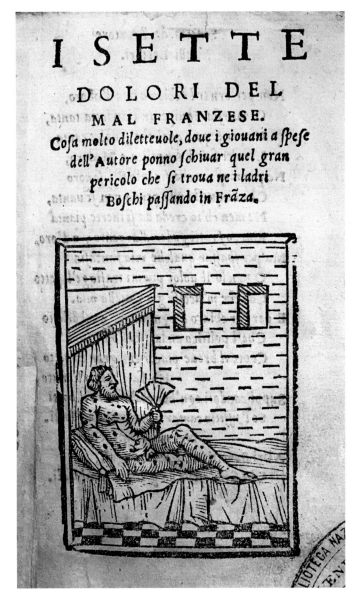

Figure 13 Andrea Veneziano (attrib.), *The Seven Pains of the French Disease,*
Frontispiece (Venice, 1555), (Ministero della Cultura/Biblioteca Nazionale
Marciana, Venice.)

the development of the third main source of pain (*Sette dolori*, 1580, verses
7–10), loss of teeth and sense of taste, returning the sufferer to being like
a *puttino* or baby, who can only eat soups. But this is not all, for the fourth
stage led to the development of 'delightful' boils: 'On your face they flower like

Figure 14 Bald man holding his hair which has fallen out
(late sixteenth century), (BCAP, MS G61, c. 33r)

roses, and make you into a beautiful person' (*Sette dolori*, 1580, verse 12).[22]
In the next phase, the disease entered the bones and led to a 'cruel pain', leading
the patient to yell and cry aloud, as gummata ate away the flesh, even on the soles
of the feet, making it incredibly difficult to walk. Finally, the pains became
'atrocious', caused by the 'cursed sore from hell', which led to death (*Sette dolori*,
1580, verses 14–16). Some idea of his appearance can be gained from the only too
graphic image in the twelfth watercolour of the Perugian manuscript (Figure 14).

This 'featherless starling' certainly looks bemused as he stares at lengths of
his own brown hair in his right hand, and his illness is reflected in the red
discolourations and ulcers on his neck, face and arms, as well as bloody
bandages on his right arm to cover his sores.

The poem describes the seven stages in the development of Mal Francese in
unflinching detail, dwelling on the growing levels of pain from being 'wretched
and cruel' as it enters the head and temples to 'torments' as it removes facial hair to
that associated with the decay and falling out of teeth to the rose-like boils and

---

[22] 'Seguitan poi le bolle dilettose,
Che del Francese ti danno corona,
Nel viso fioriran come le rose,
E ti faranno una bella persona'.

'cruel pains' as the disease enters the bones and finally to 'atrocious pain' and death. Although the intent was a cruel ridicule of the disease, the author was careful in his use of terminology, reflecting how the symptoms were described by other contemporaries, including doctors. His precise account of the malady's development suggests that even if the writer had not experienced it himself, he was an attentive observer of the suffering of others. He reflects, moreover, the accounts of the medical writers already examined, from Massa to Fracastoro, who emphasised the intolerable pains, pustules and loss of hair.

The French Disease remained a constant theme of the circle of burlesque poets associated with the relaxed atmosphere of the literary academies (Ciccarella, 2018–19, ch. 3). Giovan Francesco Bini, for example, who was a member of the society of the Intronati in Siena, published his *Chapter on the French Disease* (*Capitolo sopra il Mal Francese*), in 1530–32.[23] Antonfrancesco Grazzini, best known as 'Il Lasca', was known for his many ribald songs, particularly about his associations with courtesans, as he recorded in a letter to Lionardo Della Fonte where he mentioned 'mal francioso': as a result of 'playing around and whoring', he 'discovered two small boils at the end of his penis'. The moral of the story was: 'How much passion I seemed to have, how much pain I feel' (Grazzini, 1882 ed., 143–4; Zanrè, 2005).

This section concludes by examining another literary source, the lively and often scurrilous autobiography of the celebrated sculptor and goldsmith, Benvenuto Cellini, which he wrote in 1558. He, like the members of the literary academies, wrote a short account of his experience of Mal Francese, from which he had allegedly suffered some thirty years earlier, by which time the disease was well established and treatments had evolved from mercury to fumigation to guaiacum (Cellini, 1971 ed.,117–118).

> It is true indeed that I had got this sickness; but I believe I caught it from that lovely young servant-girl whom I was keeping when my house was robbed. The French Disease remained dormant in me for over four months before it showed itself, and then it broke out all over my body in one go. It was not like what one commonly observes, but it looked like my body was covered with certain red blisters, of the size of *quattrini* (farthings). The doctors would not call it the French Disease, although I told them why I thought it was that. I went on treating myself according to their methods, but derived no benefit. At last, then, I decided on taking the wood, against the advice of the leading physicians in Rome; and I took it, with the greatest discipline and abstinence that could be conceived. After a few days, I felt much better, with the result that after fifty days I was cured and as sound as a fish.

This description reflects the tone of much of Benvenuto's *Vita*, emphasising his sense of being a victim of circumstances. His brief sketch of the course of the

---

[23] On Bini see: http://www.treccani.it/enciclopedia/giovanni-francesco-bini_(Gianni Ballistreri: Dizionario-Biografico, 10 (1986).

disease reflected observations of doctors at the time, with a four-month period of dormancy (Fracastoro, 1930 ed., 237, 137). His claim that these swellings were not the same as those he had seen in other cases suggests a familiarity with the symptoms, which convinced him that he, as the patient, knew better than the doctors, for they had disputed his diagnosis of the Great Pox. Then Cellini, though initially adopting the treatment they prescribed, rapidly rejected it, instead taking a course of Guaiacum, which supposedly cured him.

By rejecting the medical experts' diagnosis and treatment, he emphasised his own expertise and experience, which is also reflected in the seriousness with which he followed the regime during the Holy Wood cure, 'with scrupulous discipline and rules of abstinence'. His critical attitude to doctors is also revealed in an earlier passage where he describes the role of Jacopo Berengario da Carpi (Cellini, 1971, 17–118):

> This able man in the course of his other practice took on the most desperate cases of the French Disease. In Rome this kind of illness is very partial to priests, and especially to the richest of them. When therefore Maestro Jacopo had made his talents known, he professed to work miracles in the treatment of such cases by means of certain fumigations, but he only undertook a cure after stipulating his fees, which he reckoned not by tens but by hundreds of crowns. … He was a person of great sagacity, and did wisely leave Rome, for not many months afterwards, all the patients he had treated grew so ill that they were a hundred times worse off than before he came. He would certainly have been murdered if he had remained.

Berengario was a renowned physician and anatomist who had taught at Bologna University and had been invited to treat the Pope, an honour which belies Cellini's claim the Roman clergy considered him a charlatan (French, 1985). This account, apart from making a good story supporting Cellini's suspicion of physicians, reflects his dislike of the mercurial fumigations favoured by Berengario, which by the 1530s had already gone out of fashion and their place taken by Holy Wood. The extent to which we can take Cellini's account at face value needs to be questioned, given that the *Vita* was written with the benefit of thirty years' hindsight. This episode serves as another dramatic narrative device representing the many challenges of his life, including treachery, imprisonment and accusations of murder. If escaping the clutches of the Great Pox can be seen as equivalent to escaping from prison, nonetheless his account does reflect knowledge of the disease, its symptoms and treatment.

3.3 Conclusion

While the authors of this range of sources wrote from different standpoints, whether genuinely reflecting their own experience, as with Ser Tommaso or members of the Ferrarese court, or allegedly autobiographical accounts by satirical writers or Cellini, what emerges above all is a vivid recreation of the physical suffering of patients with Mal Francese. The descriptions are considerably more detailed than those of chronicles examined in Section 1, which reflected only a very general knowledge of the disease among a wider public. The vocabulary of the later writers reflected more closely that of medical treatises (Section 2), though lacking their detailed explanatory theoretical framework. The Perugian watercolours, on the other hand, provide a visual counterpart to these descriptions, showing the effects of the disease on the human body and the emotional and facial reactions of the patient, most of whom were young men. The next section turns to examine the impact of the disease on women, and in particular courtesans and prostitutes, through the lens of another genre of popular burlesque and satirical narrative, to explore further how they reflected lay understanding of medical ideas and the wider social and moralistic implications of contracting the Pox.

4 Pox and Prostitution

4.1 Introduction

The previous section examined the real and imagined impact of the Great Pox on male sufferers. One of the striking features of these accounts is that authors often avoided stating how they had contracted the disease or their culpability, unless, as with Cellini, it served his narrative. By contrast, the satirical poems and plays about the lives of prostitutes, which became increasingly popular from the 1520s, contained a central message of moral and physical decline.

As we have seen in previous sections, early accounts of the epidemic, whether lay or medical, tended to provide a range of explanations for the origins and transmission of the disease, from astrological to corrupt air. However, some also add sexual transmission as a cause, specifically making the connection between Pox, prostitution and women more broadly. One wrote 'women have it in their nature', another that '[t]he beginning of this disease was detected from the woman's vulva', and another: 'it's caught by frequenting women who have these diseases' (Section 1; Corradi, 1884, 346, 361). This association is not surprising given the long-standing belief in the relationship between women and disease in contemporary medical theory. While men's humoural make-up was hot and dry and therefore more resistant to disease, a woman was seen as damp and cool making her more susceptible to infection (Schleiner, 1994, 500–6). As the influential medieval text, Trotula's *Book on the Diseases of Women*, had it: 'Because women are by nature weaker than men ... diseases very often abound in them especially around the organs devoted to Nature' (Green, 2001, 65).

These medical explanations ran parallel to medieval theological views of women as the heirs of Eve in her role as temptress of Adam and responsible for the Fall, lending a moral dimension to her role as an agent of contagion, and in particular in the transmission of venereal disease, as was clear from ideas concerning the nature of medieval lepra. In fact, within two years of the beginning of the initial outbreak of the Pox, Fileno delle Tuatte of Bologna labelled the new disease as the 'lepra of Saint Job', alluding to their shared symptoms of spots, ulcers and disfigurement. There was, moreover, a belief shared by doctors that lepra was caused by coitus with leprous women or intercourse during menstruation (Jacquart and Thomasset, 1985, 177–88; Rawcliffe, 2006, 48–56, 78–89). Lepra, then, lent a model for contemporaries to understand the nature of the Great Pox and it helped to shape attitudes towards those who caught and suffered from it. But there were also considerable differences, not least the scale and rapidity of spread of the Great Pox, compared with lepra, and the fact that the latter was seen as transmitted in a variety of ways, while the former was increasingly seen as a sexually contagious disease.

Ideas and explanations about the nature of the Great Pox built on these medical and theological ideas about women and played a decisive role in a shift in attitudes and policies towards prostitution in the sixteenth century along with broader social and theological changes. There was a long tradition in the Catholic Church of toleration of prostitution as a necessary evil, reflected in Thomas Aquinas's statement in his *On the Government of Rulers*, that if one removes the cesspit, the palace will become an unclean and evil-smelling place. However, the increase of physically decayed Pox patients added to the large number of diseased and disabled beggars on the streets of renaissance Europe; this led to growing intolerance and increased emphasis on the links between moral and physical decline. Luther's characterisation of the papacy as a sink of iniquity and vice following his 1510–11 visit to Rome was given extra force by the topos of the Pox-ridden prostitute. This image was popularised by Erasmus in his *Colloquies* (1518), where he developed the analogy between the corrupt diseased body of the priest and the decay of church and society, taken further by his friend, the humanist knight Ulrich von Hutten in his well-known 1519 treatise on the Pox and guaiacum (Munger, 1949; Healy, 2001, 139–143; Stein, 2006, 629).

In Italy, changing attitudes towards prostitution, immorality and disease were reflected in satirical plays and poems. As Tessa Storey has pointed out, three different types of narratives evolved across the century (Storey, 2008, ch. 1). The first took the form of a small booklet in verse, describing the rise and fall of a courtesan, sometimes prefaced by frontispieces of crude woodcuts illustrating her physical decline. Secondly, broadsheets appeared from the later sixteenth century with a single image showing the life cycle of a courtesan, as they were punished for immorality by falling ill. A third phase came with a series of images narrating a moral story, warning courtesans or their clients not to trust each other. At the same time, and following the Counter-Reformation, the church placed renewed emphasis on the role and sanctity of the family and mounted a crusade to rescue fallen women and to protect vulnerable girls from a life of sin (Rosenthal, 1992, ch. 1; McGough, 2011; Pullan, 2016). This section, then, revisits key aspects of this narrative literature through the lens of contemporary medical understanding of the Great Pox.

4.2 Pox and Prostitution in Renaissance Rome

One of the earliest and best-known poems in this genre was the *Purgatory of the courtesans of Rome* (*Purgatorio delle cortigiane di Roma*, 1529). The poem was by Maestro Andrea Veneziano, a painter and poet at the papal court, and was followed by a short sequel, *The Lament (Il Lamento)*, probably by Andrea's friend, Pietro Aretino. Both were well-known for satirical verse, building on the tradition of songs performed during carnival, the festival of public enjoyment before Lent. In these carnival songs (*canti carnascialeschi*) courtesans were portrayed either very positively or very negatively. The two authors shared a mixture of cruelty, moralising and the burlesque (Kurz, 1952, 137–9; Kunzle, 1973; Shemek, 2004, 50; Geschwind, 2010, 125–7; Storey, 2008, 25–7; Ugolini, 2009, 4; Ciccarella, 2018–19, ch. 4; Strocchia and Kelly, 2022, 10–12). These pamphlets are part of the explosion of cheap printed works that circulated from the late fifteenth century, enabling the popular poems, plays and prophecies recited in the open air and in literary academies to reach a much wider audience. Related woodcuts were often displayed in taverns and were increasingly available as single sheet broadsheets from the second half of the sixteenth century (Niccoli, 1990; Salzberg, 2010).

Although the *Purgatorio* was a satire, it also hid a more serious warning to prostitutes and prospective clients of the dangers to their health and fortune. The courtesan was warned 'not to trust in your beauty, that is brief and fragile like smoke and wind', for if now 'you are young, beautiful and clean', in old age you will be 'dressed in every misery', ending up sick in the 'new Purgatory' of the hospital of San Giacomo for incurables in Rome. The title is apt since it references that state after death of suffering, where people purified their souls by doing penance for their sins to make them worthy of entering heaven (Ugolini, 2009, 18).

Andrea recited the text during Carnival on 10 February 1525, and according to the title of the mid sixteenth-century Sienese edition of the pamphlet,

Figure 15 Andrea Veneziano, *Purgatory of the courtesans of Rome*, frontispiece (Bologna, 1529), (BNCF, Palatino, E.6.6.153.II.8), (Ministero della Cultura/ Biblioteca Nazionale Centrale Firenze)

the author 'was dressed as a beggar supported by a crutch and carrying a bell'. In a woodcut illustration on the frontispiece of a 1529 Bolognese edition (Figure 15), Andrea rests in the countryside, surrounded by flowers, while he leans on a large staff, wearing little except a wreath of laurel leaves around his midriff.

The event was staged in front of a large crowd near the River Tiber in the presence of Andrea's patron, Pope Clement VII, and his court. One of the more dramatic features of the occasion was described in an anonymous letter written to the Florentine politician, Paolo Vettori, the Admiral of the papal fleet, who was based at Civitavecchia on the coast north of Rome (Graf, 1888, 256):

> Yesterday Maestro Andrea the painter made a cart on which were papier-
> maché effigies of all the old courtesans of Rome, each one labelled with her
> name, and he threw the whole lot into the river in the presence of the Pope. He
> has sent to Orsolina the sonnet and poem which were recited. The next day the
> courtesans, to revenge themselves, beat the said Maestro Andrea through the
> streets of Rome.

Although there was no more detail concerning the appearance of the effigies, they probably mirrored the description in the poem of the effects of poverty and disease on the appearance of older prostitutes, and identifying the labels on the effigies would have further damaged their reputation. This episode underlines the agency of the courtesans themselves, as emphasised in recent literature on prostitutes in this period, for they were not powerless to demonstrate their outrage. One should also remember that all these events took place during carnival, which traditionally provided a brief period when people could protest within the safety valve of the world turned upside down.

The representation of the aged courtesans as effigies and the oral recitation was designed as a warning of the ultimate fate of any woman who became a prostitute, but significantly the poem focussed on the Ospedale di San Giacomo, which was described as a living purgatory. Here patients were described as doing penance for their sins through the sufferings of their diseased bodies; their sicknesses and symptoms are described in excruciating detail. What then does the *Purgatorio* add to our knowledge of the hospital as discussed in Section 2.4 and of their patients? In his satirical poem, Andrea began by contrasting the hospital's 'beautiful cloisters' with the physical condition of the sick, who suffered from 'pain exceeding any torment and infernal plague' (*Purgatorio*, 1529, lines 16–21: Ugolini, 2009, 17–18). He also portrayed the hospital as overcrowded and insufficient for the demand of potential patients, since, as emphasised in Leo X's papal Bull of fourteen years earlier, Rome had become full of incurables. Beds in the wards were packed closely side by side, and the beautiful cloisters had become the place where the most seriously ill were abandoned.

Given the intention to emphasise the purgatorial nature of San Giacomo, Andrea described the nature of patients' symptoms in detail. This was the place to see 'scary monsters', destroyed by their illnesses, which included lepra, cancers and 'universal sicknesses', 'that destroy the flesh down to the bone' (*Purgatorio*, 1529, lines 16–21: Ugolini, 2009, 17–18). But Andrea concen-trated mainly on Mal Francese, given its association with courtesans. The symptoms correspond quite closely to those described by medical writers, reflecting the diffusion of knowledge of the details of the disease beyond the world of practitioners. Patients suffered from pains, boils and sores, which spread from head to foot, and led to the flesh of limbs being eaten away and to losing features on their faces, including eyes, making them no longer recognisable. Then, as mentioned in Section 2.4, Leo X's *Bull* of 1515 underlines the bodily decay of the sick beggars, which generated pus and stench, leading to the corruption of the air associated with the spread of disease (*Purgatorio*, 1529, lines 50–5: Ugolini, 2009, 18):

> Full of sores from the head to the soles of the feet
> For their sins and for your example,
> Whose flesh has been all-consumed
> To the bone with rot and stench
> And as ye already were beautiful and gallant,
> Now you suffer a bitter martyrdom of sores and pain.

This satirical poem also had a serious intent, to warn women of the perils of prostitution, and to deter potentially vulnerable girls from entering the profession (Matthews Grieco, 1997, 78–86; McGough, 2011, ch. 4; Geschwind, 2012, 107–33). These themes related to a longer theological tradition, which viewed women's bodies as the primary agent of original sin, leading to both physical and moral sickness (Green 2001; Ugolini, 2009, 5–12; Ciccarella, 2018–19, ch. 4; Gagné, forthcoming). In both literary and visual portrayals, the female body disfigured by disease was contrasted with the beauty of the ideal Renaissance body, as underlined here: 'And such a one who had high and divine features now is incurably ill, like a monster' (*Purgatorio*, 1529, lines 46–7: Ugolini, 2009, 18). More specifically, some scholars suggest that this was a way of representing the lack of male responsibility for the transmission of the Great Pox (Shemek, 2004, 55–7; Zanrè, 2005, 189–91). Paola Ugolini offers a more nuanced interpretation, arguing that 'the text seems to establish a double satirical focus that does not only aim at courtesans, but at male suiters too' (Ugolini, 2009, 13–14). The fact that Andrea presented himself as a beggar with a crutch reflects the common image of those suffering from the Great Pox, whether male or female.

A further graphic representation of the later stages of the disease is shown in the crude woodcut on the title page of the edition of c. 1560 (Figure 16). A courtesan is wheeled along on a handcart, after her limbs had been attacked and weakened by the disease. Her legs are badly ulcerated, and the abscesses smelt, since they attracted flies, which she attempts to whisk away with a twig. These handcarts were a common contrivance to enable a crippled man or woman to travel around the city, as reflected in an incised marble plaque on the wall beside the entrance door to the hospital church of Santa Maria in Porta Paradisi (Figure 17). He is scantily dressed and, like the courtesan, his head is covered to hide his baldness, while his right-hand foot was probably reduced to

PVRGATORIO DELLE COR-
tegiane di Roma. Con un lamento di una
Cortigiana che fu gia fauorita poi uenu-
ta in calamtia per il mal Francese,
ſi conduſſe andare in Caretta.

AHime ſon gia ſio penſo piu giornate
chio uo gridando fate un po di bene
del Purgatorio a lanime dannate
Ma poi ch'ho ſentit'io che fra uoi ene
Purgatorio di uiui hai che dolore
ch'eccede ogni ſupplitio e infernal pene
Da pieta moſſo uengo hor con feruore
a ricordarui un nuouo Purgatorio

Figure 16 Andrea Veneziano, *Purgatory of the courtesans of Rome*
(Rome, c. 1560), (British Library Board, shelfmark:11427.b.61: frontispiece).

a stump. He is sitting in his cart with his hands joined in supplication begging
for himself and to raise funds for the hospital behind him.

This text, the *Lamento*, probably by Aretino, was recited immediately after
Andrea's *Purgatorio*, highlighted the evils associated with the social-climbing
of courtesans, reflected in the topsy-turvy world of Carnival. While Andrea
emphasised the role of San Giacomo as the purgatory for those sick with Mal
Francese, Aretino dwelt on the telling contrast between the glamorous life of
beautiful young courtesans and the poverty and ill health of their old age after
they had been afflicted with the Great Pox; this was given greater veracity as the
poem is allegedly narrated in the first person by the anti-heroine herself
(Shemek, 2004, 51–5). To underline the moral of his message, the gradual
decline of a courtesan is described, beginning with sartorial and gastronomic

Figure 17 A beggar with the Great Pox seated on a handcart, incised marble plaque, Church of S. Maria in Porta Paradisi porch, Hospital of S. Giacomo degli Incurabili, Rome (Photo: author)

contrasts between past and present (*Lamento*, in *Purgatorio*, c. 1560, ed., lines 10–18: Kurz, 1952, 164):

> I was favoured and happy,
> I wore gold, and now I wear a big sack
> I hated partridges, now I covet a root.
> I wore precious perfumes on me
> Now sulphur, mercury, impregnated evil,
> So that I can barely suffer it.
> Cabbage leaves are the beautiful tankard
> And pearls, boils, gummata, and pains,
> And I go begging a hospital [to be admitted].

Unlike the happy days when she wore gold, she now wears clothes made of sacking, and while in the past she smelt of expensive perfumes, now she smells of sulphur and mercury to treat the 'boils, gummata and pains'. Later Aretino is even more precise about the symptoms, which include first loss of eyebrows, and eventually the hair on the head, forcing her to disguise her baldness and sores with an old sheet, while her beautifully made-up face has now terrible scabs and flesh eaten-away by disease. While written in emotive language, this description reflects knowledge of the treatment of medical practitioners and their descriptions of the later stages of the disease as it disfigured the face and body (Section 2).

Decline in her health inevitably led to a gradual decline in the courtesan's standard of living, as she was forced to part with her servants, her clothes and jewellery, and her grand rooms. She is reduced to live outside in all weathers under benches, and to beg for her living on Ponte Sisto, often left without bread or warmth, until she enters the hospital of San Giacomo, where she contemplates buying poison to end her miserable existence (*Lamento*, in *Purgatorio*, c. 1560 ed., line 112).

Though satirical, and presented through the male gaze as a warning to courtesans and their clients, both poems point to the sad reality of the lives of prostitutes as they became sick with the French Disease. Andrea's image of the 'fearful monsters' must have resonated with all who had seen diseased beggars on Ponte Sisto and in other public places, and for visitors to San Giacomo and Incurabili hospitals throughout Italy. If their presence on public highways and Piazze moved some to compassion, it made others fear infection from the smell of suppurating wounds and the stinking breath which infected the air, as mentioned in a Venetian law of 1522: 'giving forth a terrible stench and infecting their neighbours and those with whom they live' (Chambers and Pullan, 1992, 308–9).

The *Purgatorio* and *Lamento* continued to be influential as models in tone and contents for the satirical and moralistic literature about the life cycle of courtesans. This can be seen in the pamphlet published some ten years later by the Florentine poet and bookseller Gianbattista Verini, *The Pride and Lament of the Ferrarese Courtesan* (*Il Vanto e Lamento della Cortegiana Ferrarese*), which places greater emphasis on her previous luxurious way of life. It enumerates the numerous attributes of her beauty, including her 'two eyes more black than crows that those who look at them are astonished', 'the lips of coral', 'the nose outlined between two roses' and 'the throat of alabaster' (*Il Vanto*, 1540, lines 13–14. 17, 20, 28).[24] She is represented as profiting from her beautiful appearance, with princes and lords paying court to her, an opulent lifestyle in a grand house, with beautiful clothes and food and wine fit for kings. After fifteen years, she began to suffer from great pains and became a 'dried leaf', leading to a bitter death (*Il Vanto*,1540, line 123). Though more emphasis is placed on what she lost than the disease, recognisable symptoms are mentioned,

---

[24] 'duoi occhi più che corbo neri che chi gli giarda resta stupefatto', 'le labra di corallo', 'el naso profilato infra due rose', 'la gola d'alabastro'.

Figure 18 Gianbattista Verini, *The pride and lament of the Ferrarese courtesan* (Siena, 1540), BNCF, Landau Finaly 535/7, frontispiece (Ministero della Cultura/Biblioteca Nazionale Centrale Firenze)

including severe pains and stench, so that 'thinking of it cracks my heart', 'so nobody will love me anymore' (*Il Vanto*, 1540, lines 125–6, 146–7).[25]

The two-part structure of the *Lamento* echoes other similar poems and plays written in Italy in the sixteenth and seventeenth centuries, contrasting the courtesan's luxurious lifestyle, with her decline and 'bitter death'. Her symptoms of pain and smell are also familiar from other contemporary descriptions, reflected in the crude print on the pamphlet's frontispiece (Figure 18). Like the woodcut accompanying the *Purgatorio*, the Ferrarese courtesan is wheeled

---

[25] 'piena son di puzze e di vil fezza, che a ciò pensando si mi crepa il cuore'; 'in pena, in pianto, in doglie acerbe amare, come parevon più no par armarme'.

along in a handcart, suggesting her difficulty in walking; but reflecting the pride of the title of the poem, she imperiously points out directions to her helper with a long, distorted finger.

4.3 The Reformation of Morals in Word and Image

Over the sixteenth century there was a general increase in intolerance towards prostitutes. Towns and cities attracted growing numbers of the marginalised poor, which included women forced into selling their bodies to survive (Storey, 2008). In Italy, the post-Tridentine Church mounted a campaign to save souls, by converting non-Christians, such as Jews and Muslims, and preventing potentially vulnerable women from becoming prostitutes. These themes were reflected in the satirical literature produced for the delectation of members of literary academies, and popularised through the explosion of print as chapbooks and broadsheets and even the text and image shown on fans. These were deliberately didactic tales, imbued with a Counter-Reformation morality (Matthews Grieco, 1997, 78–86; Storey, 2008; Geschwind, 2012; McGough, 2011, ch. 4; Strocchia, Kelly, 2022). In addition to the more traditional emphasis on the moral and physical dangers for men in associating with prostitutes, increasingly they levelled stark warnings to women of this way of life. This theme was concretely reflected in the later sixteenth-century foundation of Convertite convents to house repentant prostitutes. Although this was part of a longer tradition, the Counter-Reformation gave an extra impetus to this type of institution, as it did to those such as the Zitelle in Venice, which provided shelter to poor young women, who might otherwise, through poverty, be induced into the world of prostitution. Laura McGough has argued that the establishment of Convertite convents paralleled the foundation of Incurabili hospitals, which treated those women who had not heeded the warnings of moralists (McGough, 2011).

The admonitory message to young women of the link between prostitution, immorality and the Great Pox underlay the multiplication of popular pamphlets from the mid sixteenth century onwards with titles underlining the inevitable downward spiral of their misfortune. These included Valentino Detio il Colloredo's *The tearful and lamentable case of Cecilia Bruni from Murano* (*Caso lacrimoso e lamentevole di Cecilia Bruni Muranese, Cortegiana in Venetia a San Paterniano*), (Ronciglione, 1621), Gasparre Angeli's discourse about the courtesan Lena (Viterbo, 1622) and 'the little girl who became a courtesan through being poorly looked after by her mother' (*La putta che diventa corteggiana, Per il mal governo di sua Madre, composta da un Capriccio bizaro,* Venice, 1668). By the early seventeenth century, many texts have a different tone. They portray prostitutes as victims of their circumstances rather than as sources of moral and physical infection. Lena, for example, appears to have been fated for a misfortunate life from a young age. She was maltreated by her father, Chiappino, a cobbler on Ponte Sisto. He was murdered when Lena was nine, whereupon she was looked after by her mother, who stole from shops, though her real profession was 'to give kisses, and she provided this service to everybody' (*La putta*, 1668, lines 59–68). Lena's mother also met a grim end, being beaten so severely that she was taken to the hospital of San Giacomo, where she died two years later, after probably contracting the Great Pox. Lena, orphaned at the tender age of eleven, had little alternative but to follow the example of her mother. She shared her experience of violence and being abandoned by men with whom she had fallen in love, although the story ended happily with marriage to Zan Scarsella.

The emphasis in these stories is on a cycle of misfortune caused through no fault of the courtesan herself, but rather by the conditions in which she grew up, followed by her association with her customers who infected her with Mal Francese. This is rather a different narrative than that presented in earlier texts, such as the *Purgatorio*, where the courtesan was blamed for overweening ambition and pride, which led to her moral and physical decline.

Despite the introduction of this new more nuanced attitude, the highly moralistic genre remained strong, and the figure of the prostitute was depicted visually in a series of broadsheets, beginning with single sheets illustrating her life cycle, before developing into more complex narrative structures illustrating warnings to both prostitutes and clients of the dangers to each other.

A representative single sheet narrative is Paolo Tozzi's print dating from c. 1600, *This is the least of the sufferings of us prostitutes, dying in a hospital*, with verses adapted from a longer poem by the Venetian poet Bartolomeo Bonfante (Figure 19).

This shows the sad story of a courtesan, who, in the 'flower of my life', had been courted by gentlemen on bended knees, who sang her ballads and songs, caressed her and gave her splendid food to eat, but which all ended in tears and laments. The series of scenes reflects the remorseless turning of the wheel of fortune, as she accepts gifts and flowers from her lovers, who, though smiling, are carrying the Mal Francese. After succumbing to the embraces of one of her lovers as they lie together in the sand dunes, she begins a downward spiral, her life reduced to misery and beggary, as she is depicted with the ulcers of the Pox, while her ex-lover walks past her, holding his nose to block the smell of her disease. Intentionally or not, the posture of the courtesan echoes that of Job on the dunghill, as she is shown

Figure 19 Paolo Tozzi, *This is the least of the sufferings of us prostitutes, dying in a hospital* (verses by Bartolomeo Bonfante, c. 1600), (Civica Raccolta Stampe Achille Bertarelli, Castello Sforzesco, Milan; © Comune di Milano, all rights reserved)

semi-recumbent on a sand dune (see Section 5). She ends up sick in hospital (Ospeal), surrounded by chamber-pots and urinals, where she eventually dies. Then, as if the punishment of the pains of Mal Francese were not bad enough, the text ends with: 'After your death, you will go to the burning fire, where you will remain in perpetuity, buried in that hell.'

The complete version of Bonfante's poem is printed under a new image of c. 1620 Signora Anzola sick in hospital (Figure 20), thus returning to the topos of 100 years earlier, of the prostitute ending up in the purgatory of San Giacomo degli Incurabili in Rome. Tended by a nun, she is shown lying on a bed with her semi-nude body covered with the spots of the French Disease, reminding the viewer of the perils of the life of a prostitute. As if her suffering was not bad enough, she awaits the painful treatment of the surgeon on the left of the picture (Bonfante, 1620, verses 10–11; Kurz, 165–6):

> When the barber comes
> To undertake his trade
> And with mercury
> To caress your feet,
> He begins stressing
> You need to take off the bandages,
> And without shame
> You have to show everything
> To the one who wants to clean well,
> And so he begins
> To torment the flesh.

Figure 20 *This is the miserable end of Signora Anzola*
(Civica Raccolta Stampe Achille Bertarelli, Castello Sforzesco, Milan;

Anzola addresses the viewer with a direct glance from her sickbed, inviting us to share in her suffering, as in a later stanza she describes her painful symptoms. She is subjected to humiliating treatment by the barber, who cleans the sores all over body, presumably including her genital area, and administers ointment made from mercury sublimate, designed to eat away the sores and ulcers (Kunzle, 1973, 127–8; Storey, 2008, 28–9; Strocchia, Kelly, 2022, 15).

In the same way that satirical literature 100 years earlier had fallen into two distinct categories, the decline of courtesans and the sickness of men with Mal Francese, so these more complex narrative broadsheets can be divided into those depicting the decline of a prostitute and analogous stories of a rake. The latter emerged slightly later, but many of the textual descriptions, such as Bonfante's, and their visual counterparts had much in common, relying on one another as models. It has been argued that the Bolognese Giuseppe Maria Mitelli's 1692 etching, *La vita infelice della meretrice* (*The unhappy life of the prostitute*), may reflect an engraving by Andrea and Michelangelo Vaccari in early seventeenth-century Rome (Kurz, 1952, 145). The scenes of the prostitute's life are divided into twelve months. In January, she blithely dances away with her noble lover, accompanied by musicians, little aware of what her future has in store for her as the year progresses. The final two scenes show her decline and demise; while reflecting themes of Paolo Tozzi's print of 1600, they are transformed through a much more fluid and sophisticated rendition (Figure 21).

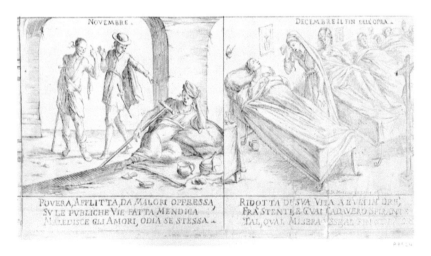

Figure 21 Giuseppe Maria Mitelli, *The unhappy life of the prostitute* (etching, 1692), (Civica Raccolta Stampe Achille Bertarelli, Castello Sforzesco, Milan; © Comune di Milano, all rights reserved)

In November, we see the familiar image of the sick prostitute reduced to begging on the street, half-lying and supported by a crutch. A young man wearing a hat, short cloak and sword, to denote his social status, points with horror at the recumbent figure, whose fate is mirrored by the accompanying beggar, who points at his head and disfigured face to emphasise the misery of the disease. The moral of the story is stated in the text underneath: 'The poor afflicted woman, oppressed by diseases, which cause her to be a beggar on the public streets, curses the lovers, hates herself.' Significantly for our theme, disease is represented through the disability of lameness, rather than a visual description of her body covered with ulcers and gummata, as it had earlier. The same remains true of the final scene, 'December and the end of the work', where she appears in her last hours lying in a hospital bed suffering 'hardships and woes' associated with the Great Pox. Her unmarked face is drawn and gaunt, and she is comforted by the crucifix at the foot of her bed and a well-dressed lady lamenting her fate.

The broadsheets and poems of narratives about the decline of both prostitutes and rakes led to the production of elaborate and multi-episode broadsheets. While the reasons that girls became courtesans had more to do with escaping poverty, for men the stories usually involved more affluent individuals, who had lost honour and riches due to their immoral activities and Mal Francese often played an important role in their downfall.

These themes sounded familiar to English and French audiences, because the topic of the connection between the French Disease and immorality was a popular theme of literature well beyond early modern Italy. Catholic corruption was echoed in *Measure for Measure*, where Shakespeare likened society to a diseased body polluting the way England was governed. In contemporary French literature, as in the writings of Rabelais, the country was portrayed as a metaphorical patient ravaged by the wars of religion (Healy, 2001, ch. 4; Losse, 2015). Italian broadsheets also inspired iconographic representations of these themes in England, most famously in William Hogarth's *A Harlot's Progress* and *A Rake's Progress*, a series of paintings and prints from the 1730s (Kurtz, 1952; Bindman,1981, 2021).

4.4 Conclusion

The popularity and constant reprinting of these pamphlets and broadsheets points to their hold on the popular imagination. Not only were they distributed widely by travelling vendors and charlatans and displayed in taverns but also scenes came to be popularised further by being reproduced on fans. Close examination of these texts and images shows that the same themes and even the same words were repeated from one pamphlet or broadsheet to another, reinforcing the underlying moral of the Catholic Church's campaign to reform morals and to remedy social and sexual failings. They also carried a warning about avoiding contact with locations of infection, whether brothels or diseased bodies.

The textual descriptions of Mal Francese, whether in the allegedly autobiographical verses of male patients or the anti-courtesan literature, provided a detailed guide to the signs and symptoms of the Great Pox, which mirrored accounts in medical treatises. The more general public was made aware of the suffering of patients through the mouths of travelling performers, while the visual images of victims added another dimension to their understanding. The boils and ulcerated pustules shown in popular prints reflected the basic symptoms of the disease, especially when linked to disfigurement of the face and limbs, as reflected in the frontispiece of the *Purgatory of Courtesans*. Emphasis is placed on the sickness of women rather than on their male clients, and while their symptoms were often represented schematically, there were clearly those of the Great Pox described in verse in the texts. The final section will return to examine the visual representation of the Pox on the male body through images of St Job, also often shown schematically, appropriate to the genre. Altarpieces and frescoes of Job reflected and diffused the moral message of the church and at the same time knowledge of the effects of the disease.

5 Pox, Religion and St Job

5.1 Introduction: Lepra and the French Disease

The image of St Job most familiar in the Middle Ages was as patron saint of 'lepra', when he was often shown covered with small spots, reflecting the description in the Book of Job 2:7 as suffering from ulcers, 'from the soles of his feet to the top of his head'. Like St Sebastian, the patron of plague, who recovered from his first martyrdom, Job offered hope to victims, since he had survived and been cured through God's grace. Many of these depictions of Job's disease were very schematic, as in Bartolo di Fredi's fresco of *Job and His Friends* (c. 1370), in the Collegiata of San Gimignano in Tuscany (Figure 22). This detail shows his almost naked body and face decorated with small brown boils, with no reference to the more developed symptoms when the disease attacked the soft tissue and bones (Terrrien, 1996; Rawcliffe, 2006; Carnevale, 2010, 2015; Boeckl, 2011, 83–5; Argenziano, 2012; Helas, 2018; Presciutti, 2021).

This section will examine the ways in which Job was depicted, and whether his iconography changed when he became patron saint of the Great Pox, a disease also typified by lesions (cf. Argenziano, 2013, 79–95). While in early printed books in

Figure 22 Bartolo di Fredi, *Job and his friends* (detail), Collegiata of San Gimignano (c. 1370), (Wikipedia Commons)

northern Europe Job appeared in scenes showing God's punishment for sexual misdemeanours, some of the earliest Italian iconography linking Job with Mal Francese concentrated instead on illustrating themes of his life, a theme which gradually gave way to representation alongside other saints associated with disease (Schleiner, 1994). We shall trace the growing popularity of his image above all in northern and central Italy, and it will be argued that his increased visibility was at least in part a response to the demand from hospitals and confraternities associated with the campaign to treat the Great Pox (see Section 2).[26] In the process we shall examine more broadly how representations of Job related to that of 'lepra' and plague; although there are many studies of the imagery of these two disease, there is no overall survey of the visual representation of the Great Pox in renaissance Italy (Lodone, 2015, 41; Boekl, 2011; Bailey et al., 2005). Part of the explanation may be that an epidemic of plague was an inherently more dramatic event than the Pox, killing large numbers of people in a short time, with the resulting need to bury thousands, while the Pox was a chronic disease and its victims suffered a long-drawn-out death (Henderson, 2013). The outward signs of the plague, with the large

---

[26] The present section presents a preliminary analysis of a small selection of a much larger database of St Job imagery from across northern and central Italy, to be developed in a longer study.

buboes under the armpits or on the thigh, were also more instantly recognisable than the generalised spread of pustules over the body.

We have met Job as patron saint of the Great Pox through references in both chronicles and the *Lament of Strascino* (Sections 1 and 3), but a brief examination of his life helps to clarify his appeal. The story of Job was familiar in the Middle Ages from The Golden Legend, the popular collection of saints' lives by the thirteenth-century Dominican, Jacopo da Voragine, and from visual representations usually in ecclesiastical contexts. The basic story addressed the question of why God permits evil in the world, and involved the central character, Job, whose personal tragedies were visited upon him by the devil as a test of his faith, including loss of worldly goods, death of offspring and skin diseases. Job's faith ultimately triumphed when he was once again returned by God to his former state. The Golden Legend introduces four more characters to tease out some of the themes of the topic: Job's wife berates him for not actively cursing God for causing his suffering, while his friends, Eliphas, Bildad and Zophar, assert he is being punished for his sins.

Job personifies patience in the face of adversity, and as an exemplar for those suffering from long-drawn-out chronic diseases. The New Testament inspiration for the iconography of 'lepra' lay in the episodes when Christ healed a leper and raised Lazarus from the dead (Boeckl, 2011, ch. 4).

From the later fourteenth century onwards, depictions of the symptoms of 'lepra' became more graphic, showing deeper ulcers and distorted limbs and noses (Boeckl, 68–9). This change is largely attributed to the resurgence of its religious importance under the influence of the Observant Franciscans, building on the legend of Francis's visit to tend patients in a leper hospital. More generally, the Observants emphasised the importance of engagement with the community through charitable works, leading the friars to inspire the foundation or re-foundation of substantial hospitals to treat the sick. These two themes are brought together in an illustration to the Perugian manuscript *La Franceschina*, a 1474 chronicle of the Order by the Franciscan Jacopo Oddi (Figure 23). In this image Francis and his companions nurse lepers, whose lesions are shown in horrific detail; green and red paints are used to depict the raised nodules and bruised skin, and the sick men have distorted bodies and faces (Presciutti, 2021, 92–5, 97).

Even with the Observant Franciscans' increased interest in lepra, visual representations of it in Italy became much more sporadic, reflecting the disease's overall decline. At the same time, Job took on his new role as patron saint of the Great Pox, and came to be known, among other names, as 'the disease of St Job'. Another epithet used by early Italian chronicles was the 'lepra of St. Job', which reflects the lack of certainty about the identity of the disease at

Figure 23 *St Francis and companions tending to lepers in a leprosarium*,
Jacopo Oddi, *La Franceschina* (1474), BCAP, MS 1238 f.223r
(Wikipedia Commons)

the beginning of the epidemic. This was in turn translated into uncertainty about its visual representation, and particularly whether symptoms depicted within the first decade referred to lepra or the French Disease, or even both. This was particularly true of early narrative of Job's life; one of the most complete cycles was by Pseudo-Bartolommeo di Giovanni. He was active in late fifteenth-century Florence and associated with Domenico Ghirlandaio, whose busy workshop produced paintings for charitable institutions, such as the foundling hospital of the Innocenti and the confraternity of the Buonomini di S. Martino (Zeri and Gardner, 1971, 140–1).

Figures 24–26 reproduce three of the five scenes. The first shows the destruction of Job's house and the death of his children, while the second and third emphasise Job's interaction with his wife and friends. In Figures 25 and 26 there is a striking contrast between his richly dressed friends and Job's almost nude body covered with a series of brown spots on his face, torso and legs. The dependence of the iconographic tradition of Job as leper can be seen clearly in the near contemporary fresco by Cosimo Rosselli in the Sistine Chapel, *Christ*

Figure 24 Pseudo-Bartolommeo di Giovanni, 'The destruction of Job's
house and the death of his children', detail of *The story of Job*
(late fifteenth century), State Museums in Berlin, Picture Gallery (Jörg P.
Anders. Public Domain Mark 1.0)

Healing a Leper, which forms part of *The Sermon on the Mount* (Boeckl, 132–
36), (Figure 27).

Figure 26 shows Job in bed, his condition having worsened with the
pustules now depicted more realistically, larger, redder and more prominent, similar to the lepers in *La Franceschina*. In this panel, the configur-
ation is slightly different; two men are accompanied by Job's wife and
a female servant. His wife, identified by a crown, is remonstrating with
Job, who holds out his hand to ward off her injudicious advice to reject
God for his unjust punishment. The identity of the two men is not clear,
though the one wearing a red head covering was probably a physician
discussing Job's condition and treatment with his colleague. The empty
bowl brought by the servant, who is looking at the physician, may indicate
imminent blood-letting, part of the therapy recommended by doctors for
both lepra and the Great Pox. The body language is similar to the depiction
of physician and apothecary in Domenico di Bartolo's fresco of the scene
in the hospital ward of Santa Maria della Scala in Siena painted in
the 1440 (Bell, 2021). The physician holds his nose indicating the smell
given off by Job's suppurating pustules, though his richly dressed compan-
ion stands on the platform surrounding the bed, reflecting the physical
relationship between patients and practitioners in the woodcut on the
frontispiece of the *Lament of Strascino* (Figure 12).

Figure 25 Pseudo-Bartolommeo di Giovanni, 'Job visited by his friends in the wilderness' (late fifteenth century), State Museums in Berlin, Picture Gallery

Figure 26 Pseudo-Bartolommeo di Giovanni, 'Job on his sickbed' (late fifteenth century), State Museums in Berlin, Picture Gallery

Figure 27 Cosimo Rosselli, *Christ healing a leper,* detail of: *The sermon on the mount* (1481–82) Sistine Chapel, Vatican City (Wikipedia Commons)

5.2 Job in the Sixteenth century

From the early sixteenth century Job usually appears as a free-standing figure, not part of a narrative, and with other saints, usually Sebastian and Rocco, patrons of plague victims. In this new iconography, more emphasis is placed on the pronounced signs of disease on his pock-marked body (Lodone, 2015, 35–43). Job's representation makes an instructive comparison with his frequent companions, Sebastian and Rocco. In common with Sebastian, he is shown as semi-nude, but they differ in age and attributes. Sebastian is portrayed as a youth with an unblemished idealised body pierced by arrows to represent his first martyrdom and the arrows of disease. Though Job also appears semi-nude, he is typically depicted as an older man covered with ulcers and sporting a long white beard. Rocco, whose cult also developed later in the fifteenth century, is shown as a young nobleman pointing to a plague bubo prominently displayed on his upper thigh. While depictions of the attributes of these plague saints remained quite standard, from the latter half of the sixteenth century there was an increasing tendency to include scenes showing the impact of epidemics on the population of cities. Dramatic images of sick and dying men, women and children appeared either in predellas of altarpieces of holy figures or as an integral part of scenes of saints, such as S. Carlo Borromeo tending to the sick (Bailey et al., 2005; Barker, 2021).

One of the earliest representations of St Job to be securely linked to Mal Francese is an altarpiece by Domenico Panetti including St Job, commissioned by a confraternity in Ferrara dedicated to St Giobbe. It had been founded in 1499 and was granted a patent by Duke Ercole d'Este to collect funds through the state to establish a hospital for incurables, reflecting that the sickness was widespread in the city and among members of the Este family (Section 3; AHF, 47, 151–2). The confraternity commissioned a series of images of the saint, the earliest of which was Panetti's *Virgin and Child with Saints Job, Antonio Abbate, Vito and Pietro Martire* (1503) designed for the high altar of the chapel, complementing a fresco-cycle of scenes from Job's life commissioned at the same time from the local artist Zohaine dall'Agnolo, (Figure 28), (Lodone, 2015, 36, 47–9, 151–2, 319, n. 32).

Panetti shows Job with joined hands in supplication on behalf of those sufferings from the French Disease, with pustules and boils on his torso, feet and lower legs. The marks are sufficiently pronounced to indicate Job's association with Pox, and may reflect an early stage of the disease, with small, dry ulcers which developed into pustules, as described by Fracastoro. Towards the end of the century, the confraternity commissioned the Ferrarese painter Ippolito Scarsellino to produce a set of eight panels illustrating *The History of Job* to replace the earlier fresco-cycle (now in the Landesmuseum, Hannover; Novelli, 2008, 112–5, 304).

Incurable hospitals and confraternities continued to commission works to adorn their churches, oratories and ward chapels, many appearing in the first quarter of the sixteenth century. Like many incurable hospitals, Santa Maria dei Guarini in Bologna, adapted a pre-existing institution, which they re-dedicated to Job.

In the case of Bologna, two strikingly different images of Job were commissioned in this period, one for the main altar of the oratory, and the other for their statutes. The first was painted in 1510 by Francesco de' Giacomo Raibolini the Bolognese artist known as il Francia, showing the crucifixion framed by the two standing figures of the Madonna and St John the Evangelist (Figure 29). Both are fully dressed, in stark contrast to the virtually nude Job on the ground in front of the cross, reflecting his traditional stance, lying on a dunghill. He points

Figure 28 Domenico Panetti, *Virgin and child with saints* (1503), Pinacoteca Nazionale, Ferrara (Creative Commons: CC-BY-4.0. https://catalogo.benicul turali.it/detail/HistoricOrArtisticProperty/0800046616)

to a banner above him on which is written 'Maiora. Sustinuit. Ipse'. The message is clear: that by carrying his cross of suffering, his faith will win in the end (Lodone, 2015, 47–8).

Though the Incurable hospital is dedicated to the treatment of Mal Francese, Job's body appears free of blemish, a stylistic decision in line with Il Francia's highly idealised figures. This is in strong contrast with how Job was depicted in the illumination to the papal privilege to the hospital in 1535. The detail depicted in Figure 30 shows Job to the left side of Mary, the Madonna of Mercy, who spreads out her blue cloak to protect the members of the flagellant confraternity. Job wears a red mantle and extends his left hand towards the flagellants, recommending them to Mary for her protection. The red sores which cover his entire body, including his face, arms and legs, are particularly striking, and remind one of some of the red lesions of patients illustrated in the Perugian

Figure 29 Il Francia, *Crucifixion with St Job* (1510), Musée du Louvre, Paris
(Wikimedia Commons: Sailko)

album. The lesions correspond to contemporary lay and medical descriptions of the symptoms in the later stages of the French Disease, but without the distorted limbs, which would probably have been considered inappropriate for the context of this image.

The iconography of both images indicates the importance of function and setting. The altarpiece, which emphasised Job's penitential role and the acceptance of suffering in the path towards physical and spiritual health, was designed for a more public audience, while the statutes would have been viewed only by members of the hospital community. The contrast between an image for a more private as opposed to a public audience was also mirrored in the vivid depiction of lepra in the *Franceschina* manuscript in comparison with the vast majority of altarpieces and frescoes of Job in the Middle Ages.

Figure 30 St Job, the Madonna della Misericordia and three confraternity members (Archivio di Stato di Bologna, Privilegio di papa Paolo III, anno 1535, in Ospedali, S. Maria dei Guerini, poi S. Giobbe, serie IV, Miscellanea, b. 2. N.8; Protocollo n. 4303 del 20/07/2023)

The cult of Job in the sixteenth century enjoyed extraordinary popularity, as reflected in the many images of the saint in northern and central Italy; an initial survey reveals over fifty paintings, including frescoes. These commissions were driven initially by hospitals and confraternities, which inspired their multiplication in conventual and parish churches. They were not just in major cities, but also in small provincial towns and remote country areas.

The new and important association of Job with Sebastian and Rocco underlines his role in protecting the sick, as reflected in the fresco-cycle commissioned by the confraternity administering a hospital, S. Antonio Abate in San Daniele dei Friuli. In 1513–22, Martino da Udine, or Pellegrino da S Daniele, and his workshop painted the church interior. The panel showing the three saints together is of particular interest because of the contrast between the way their bodies were represented, given that each was linked to a major disease (Figure 31). On our right a well-dressed Rocco gazes at the viewer with his left leg exposed to show a significant raised brown bubo to which he points with his left hand, underlining its importance as a well-known symptom of plague. On the left, the pale-skinned and virtually unblemished youthful body of Sebastian is pierced by a single arrow. In stark contrast, the older Job with a white beard has a much darker skin tone. He is semi-dressed, revealing a scattering of brown lesions on his arms and legs, distinct from Rocco's bubo (Bergamini and Barattini, 2000, 83, 86–7).

Figure 31 Pellegrino da S Daniele, workshop, *Sts Job, Sebastian and Rocco,* fresco, St Antonio Abate, San Daniele dei Friuli (1513-1522), (Photo: Kunsthistorisches Institut in Florenz – Max-Planck-Institut, detail)

Job also appears with other holy figures associated with disease, as with a commission by the confraternity of bombardiers of St Barbara in the Carmelite Church of Santa Croce in Vicenza (Figure 32).

In 1505–08, Marcello Fogolino painted this altarpiece for the Chapel of Santa Barbara, the patron saint of soldiers. It shows the enthroned Virgin and Child; St Job stands semi-nude to the Virgin's right in contrast to the richly apparelled St Gottardo. Though Gottardo was the patron saint of illnesses, such as fevers and podagra, his face and hands are unblemished, while Job's body is covered with clearly portrayed red lesions and boils. This graphic depiction of a disease well-known to its intended audience, for soldiers initially spread it through Italy, recalls the Perugian watercolour of the army surgeon treating a man with severe red lesions (Figure 7). The altarpiece also underlined Job's patience in the face of suffering as he prays to the Virgin and Christchild (Lucco, 1990, 309–311; Lodone, 2015, 51).

We began this section by asking how far the representation of the French Disease in relation to Job differed from the iconography of lepra on his body and that of Lazarus. While the more decorative presentation had much more in common with the traditional representation of Job's 'lepra', ulcers and pustules of the Great Pox were more distinctive.

Interpreting the representation of disease in the visual arts is no more straight-forward than in the literary context, discussed in Sections 3 and 4. Fortunately, an

Figure 32 Marcello Fogolino, *Madonna and child with Sts Job and Gottard* (1505–08): Pinacoteca di Brera, Milan (Creative Commons: CC-BY-4.0) (https://catalogo.beniculturali.it/detail/HistoricOrArtisticProperty/00180074)

altarpiece by Francesco Pagani for the convent of San Francesco in Conegliano in the northern Veneto in the 1520s offers a comparison between Job and Lazarus (Figure 33). Both men appear semi-nude, but Job's body, discretely covered with a branch and leaves, has a scattering of brown ulcers. The only indication of Lazarus's sickness is the dog licking his sore ankle. Of course, the main purpose of the altarpiece was not medical illustration, even though sickness is represented, but religious and is reflected in the moving and intense Franciscan piety, with the dead Christ supported by Mary's arms and the two saints.

We have seen that the first forty years of the sixteenth century often saw greater attention paid to depiction of the symptoms of the Great Pox, reflecting wider knowledge of the disease not only among those who commissioned images, including confraternities, hospitals and the Franciscans, but also among members of the wider public. Another temporal change from the later

Figure 33 Francesco Pagani detto da Milano, *The descent from the cross with the Virgin, and Sts Job and Lazarus* (1520s), Gallerie dell'Accademia, Venice (BCS: LICENCE CC-BY 4.0)

sixteenth century was a return to narrative scenes. The importance of narrative was reflected in Gregory Martin's 1581 guidebook *Roma Sancta*, describing a scene in front of the Roman Incurabili hospital of San Giacomo on their main feastday: 'Upon St James day in Julie, when al the citie visiteth this Hospital, there are set forth in lively purtraicts Job with his sores upon the dunghill, his wife holding her nose for niceness not abiding her husband's stinche, his three frenddes weeping and lamenting his case' (Martin, 1969 ed., 187; AHF, ch. 8).

The display of these images was intended to solicit both compassion for the sufferings of the poor incurables and financial support for the hospital. Figure 34, a later print of a 1622 altarpiece, summarises many of the themes discussed in Section 3.2. It is by the Sienese painter Raffaello Vanni and is a dramatic transposition of the traditional scene of Job being mocked by his wife into the battle between good and evil, reflecting the woodcut on the title page of the *Lament* of *Strascino* (Figure 12). The semi-clad Job is shown seated on the base of a neo-classical column. Though his wife urges him to abandon God, as indicated by Job's glowing halo, his battle against temptation is nearly over. Evil has been overcome, as one can see from the devil's upended body with taloned

Figure 34 Raffaello Vanni, *St Job mocked by his wife* (late eighteenth-century
print of 1622 altarpiece), (Wellcome Collection: Public Domain)

legs and feet at the very centre of the composition, while Job glances towards
the heavens and God reaches out to save him. This picture, then, paints a strong
moral and theological message, underlined by the important, if subtle, role of
the depiction of disease. If not as dramatic as some of the earlier sixteenth-
century images of the saint, nevertheless his body was marked by a series of
lesions, which would have been recognisable, in conjunction with this narrative,
as representing the French Disease. There may be a number of reasons to
explain this iconographic shift to moralising themes. It may reflect changing
priorities and tastes following the Counter-Reformation. As we have seen in
Section 4, less emphasis was placed on the close connection between disease
and sin and more on redeeming fallen women and discouraging young women
becoming involved in prostitution. Literary texts came to place more emphasis
on immorality with less discussion of the detailed symptoms of disease. In the
cheap woodcuts and prints detailing the remorseless wheel of fortune associated

with the decline of women who sold their bodies, the French Disease became a symbol of wider social and moral malaise.

5.3 Conclusion

This section has underlined the growing popularity of the cult of Job in sixteenth-century Italy, as images of the saint in altarpieces and fresco-cycles penetrated major cities and towns and smaller and more isolated rural areas. Many images of Job were commissioned for chapels and churches belonging to hospitals and confraternities associated with the treatment of the French Disease, but they also spread out to parish churches and religious Orders, particularly Franciscans.

Broadly, the way that the French Disease was represented grew out of Job's earlier role as patron of 'lepra', and while there were many similarities, particularly in the rather schematic representation of symptoms, some distinct traits of ulcers and pustules did emerge, which reflected descriptions of the Great Pox by medical and lay writers. There was also much variation in how the disease was shown according to the context of a commission. Patrons might wish the artist to stress Job's role as a penitential saint who was to be emulated, but with less stress on symptoms and more on suffering to be emulated, while in others, such as in hospital contexts, ulcers and pustules were shown in greater detail to emphasise how a patient needed faith to recover. The return to more narrative scenes in the later sixteenth century, reflecting wider shifts in religious and moral discourse, meant that Job's symptoms remained an integral if more subtle part of his iconography.

Conclusion

This Element has provided a fresh approach to the study of the impact of the French Disease in Renaissance Italy by re-examining textual and visual sources through the perspective of contemporary medical accounts of the disease. It builds on the research of medical, social, literary and art historians to throw new light on a wide range of written and pictorial evidence. The analysis of written texts, from medical treatises and chronicles to plays and poems, together with visual sources of handbills, broadsheets and images of St Job, has shown how medical ideas about the nature and symptoms of the Great Pox were received and understood by a wider public and how they shifted over the sixteenth century.

Discussion of the representation and reception of the French Disease has shown how knowledge about the ways in which it affected the human body travelled almost as quickly as the disease itself. Chroniclers provided a guide for the literate public to its symptoms and impact on society, mirroring the general characteristics described by medical writers at the time. It was the increasing availability of cheap print following the recent invention of the printing press that led to the wider spread of knowledge about the Great Pox across Europe. In Italy, images of poxed bodies multiplied from the early decades of the sixteenth century through crude woodcuts accompanying the popular satirical literature about the life and decline of prostitutes. They gained further visibility when displayed in taverns, alongside handbills of prognostications and advertisements for charlatans' nostrums. From mid-century these simple images were supplemented by broadsheets, illustrating in greater detail the lives of prostitutes and their clientele. These prints and texts were by their nature misogynistic and critical of the life of courtesans, but they educated the public about the basic symptoms of the Great Pox and how it was transmitted.

This genre also served as a warning both to men from frequenting prostitutes and to young girls from becoming involved in the sex trade. The moralistic character of the literature on the Pox and prostitution, with women seen as transmitters of disease, was further strengthened by the Counter-Reformation's campaign to reform the morals of society. In Protestant Europe, writers employed the trope of immorality as a weapon in the propaganda war against Catholicism. Figures like Erasmus, Luther and Calvin, portraying the papacy as a whore, and the Great Pox as a symbol of the physical and moral corruption of the Catholic Church, reflected more generally in contemporary books and plays, most famously by Rabelais and Shakespeare.

In contrast, the moralistic strain was often lacking in medical treatises or even in male autobiographical literature, which, whether real or imagined, provided a more personal picture of the impact of the Pox on the male body, as in the case of Campani and Cellini. Authors recounted in agonising detail the stages in the disease's development, reflecting descriptions in treatises by physicians and surgeons. Many of these satirical writers came into contact with doctors at noble and papal courts, and, as we have seen at the Este court in Ferrara and Mantua, they mixed with their noble patrons, who themselves had developed the disease. Less remains known about genuinely personal experience, and further analysis is needed of letter collections and diaries, to build up a more complete idea of the lay understanding of the French Disease. This type of source also throws light on the strategies of patients in coping with their symptoms and the range of practitioners they consulted, from physicians and surgeons to male and female empirics.

This Element is among the first studies to foreground the visual representation of the French Disease from a variety of perspectives, in contrast to the many studies of 'lepra' and plague in the Middle Ages and Renaissance. It has been underlined that the way the French Disease was depicted carried different messages depending on the function of the medium. The popular woodcuts and broadsheets in the life of prostitutes aimed to show the devastating effects of

Mal Francese, leading to terrible physical sickness and death as part of a moral message to discourage women and men from indulging in illicit sex. However, the disease was presented in a very schematic way, very different from the vivid watercolours from Perugia, which instead provided detailed and arresting depictions of the impact of the disease on the body. Remarkably, these images also reflect the reactions of patients to the symptoms as they were described in medical and literary texts, as they are shown yelling out in agony at the effect of both the disease and of the doctors' treatment.

Symptoms also appeared in the emergent genre of images of St Job, associated closely with the Great Pox. As with satirical illustrations accompanying courtesan literature, the boils and abscesses on his body were often represented in a rather schematic fashion, following the tradition of painted or sculpted images of 'lepra' and plague in the Middle Ages. Even so, it would have been clear to those who prayed to Job for relief, that these were the signs and symptoms of the Great Pox. Job brings together a number of themes of this study, as he struggled with the notions of guilt and punishment, even if unfairly levelled against him, as well as the idea of penitence, as he suffered on his dunghill. Future research will examine further the imagery of the French Disease in frescoes and altarpieces of St Job. More broadly, there is much to be learned from the approaches of recent studies of depiction of disease in this period and how and why their representation varied according to the context and the type and function of the medium.

References

Manuscript Sources

Archivio di Stato di Bologna, Archivio degli Ospedali, S. Maria dei Guarini e S. Giobbe, ser IV.

Archivio di Stato di Firenze, Ospedale di Santa Maria Nuova.

Biblioteca Communale Augusta di Perugia: MS G61: 'Figure diverse di malfrancesati', late sixteenth century.

: MS 1238: Jacopo Oddi, 'La Franceschina', 1474

British Museum 197*.d.2: 'Album of watercolours of botanical, medical, mythological and biblical subjects', c. 1560.

Printed Sources

Angeli, Gasparre. (1622). *Il discorso di Lena cortiggiana, con il suo maritaggio con Zan Scarsella*. Ronciglione: Lodovico Grignani e Lorenzo Lupis.

Benivieni, Antonio. (1954). *De abditis nonnullis ac mirandis morborum et sanitorium causis*, Trans., Charles Singer. Springfield: C. C. Thomas.

Bonaini, Francesco, ed. (1845). 'Memoriale di Giovanni Portoveneri dall'anno 1494 sino al 1502'. *Archivio Storico Italiano* 6.2, 281–360.

Bonaini, Francesco, Luigi Polidori, eds. (1851). '*Cronaca della città di Perugia dal 1492 al 1503 di Francesco Matarazzo detto Maturanzio*', *Archivio Storico Italiano* 16.2.

Campani, Niccolò. (1523). *Il lamento di quell tribolato di Strascino*. Venice: Nicolo Zopino e Vincentio compagno.

Campani, Niccolò. (1564). Il *lamento di quel tribolato di Strascino Campana Senese sopra il male incognito el qual tratta di patientia et impatientia*. Venice: Francesco de Leno.

Cavriolo, Elia. (1585). *Delle historie bresciane di M. Helia Cavriolo*. Brescia: Marchetti.

Chambers, David, Brian Pullan, eds. (1992). *Venice: A Documentary History, 1450–1630*. Oxford: Basil Blackwell.

Corradi, Alfonso, ed. (1884). 'Nuovi documenti per la storia delle malattie veneree in Italia dalla fine del Quattrocento alla metà del cinquecento', *Annali universali di medicina e chirurgia* 269, 289–386.

Da Voragine, Jacopo. (1996). *The Golden Legend*. https://sourcebooks.fordham.edu/basis/golden/20legend/GoldenLegend-Volume2.asp.

Della Croce, Giovanni Andrea. (1583). *Cirugia uniuersale e perfetta di tutte le parti pertinenti*. Venice: Giordano Ziletti.

Detio, Valentino, detto Colloredo. (1621). *Caso lacrimosa e lamentevole di Cecilia Bruni Muranese,cortegiana in Venetia a San Paterniano*. Ronciglione: Lodovico Grignani e Lorenzo Lupis.

Eatough, Geoffrey, trans. (1984). *Fracastoro's 'Syphilis'* . Liverpool: Francis Cairns.

Ferrero, Giuseppe Guido, ed. (1971). *Opere di Benvenuto Cellini*. Turin: UTET.

Fioravanti, Leonardo. (1561). *De Capricci medicinali*. Venice: Lodovico Avanzo.

Fracastoro, Girolamo. (1950). *Il contagio, le malattie contagiose e la loro cura*, ed., Vincenzo Busacchi. Florence: Leo S. Olschki.

Fracastoro, Girolamo. (1930). *De contagione et contagiosis morbis et eorum curatione libri tres*, ed. & trans., Wilmer Cave Wright. New York: G. P. Putnam's Sons.

Fracastoro, Girolamo. (1939). *Trattato inedito in prosa di Girolamo Fracastoro sulla sifilide*, ed., Francesco Pellegrini. Verona: Tipografica Veronese.

Fumi, Luigi II, ed. (1925). 'Diario di Ser Tommaso di Silvestro in Ephemerides Urbevetanae dal Codice Vaticano Urbinate 1745 (AA. 1482–1514)'. *Rerum Italicarum Scriptores* 15.5. Bologna: Nicola Zanichelli.

Grazzini, Antonfrancesco. (1882). *Le rime burlesque*i, ed., Carlo Verzone. Florence: Sansoni.

Guicciardini, Francesco. (1971). *Storia d'Italia*. I, ed., S. Seidel Menchi. Turin: Einaudi.

Il Grappa. (1545). *I cicalamenti del Grappa intorno al sonetto*. Mantua: B. Canovetti.

La putta che diventa corteggiana, Per il mal governo di sua madre, composta da un capriccio bizaro. (1668). Venice: A.Z.

Landucci, Luca. (1985). *Diario Fiorentino dal 1450 al 1516*. Florence: Sansoni.

Martin, Gregory. (1969). *Roma Sancta, 1581*, ed., George Bruner Parker. Rome: Storia e letteratura.

Massa, Niccolò. (1566). *Il libro del mal francese, composto dall'Eccell. Medico, & Filosofo M. Niccolò Massa Venetiano, Nuouamente tradotto da un dottissimo Medico, di Latino, nella nostra lingua Italiana*. Venice: Giordano Ziletti.

Pellegrini, Francesco, ed. (1939). *Trattato inedito in prosa di Gerolamo Fracastoro sulla sifilide*. Verona: Tipografica Veronese.

Rostinio, Pietro. (1565). *Trattato del mal francese … nel quale si discorre sopra CCXXXIIII sorti di detto male*. Venice: Giorgio de'Cavalli.

Stefani, Federico, ed. (1879). *I diarii di Marino Sanuto, MCCCCXCVI-MDXXXIII*. Venice: F. Visentini, Vol. I.

Veneziano, Andrea. (1529). *Purgatorio delle cortigiane di Roma*. Bologna: ad istantia di Joan Maria Lirico Venitiano.

Veneziano, Andrea (attrib,). (1555). *Li sette dolori di Mal Franzese*. Venice: Schiarra compagni.

Veneziano, Andrea (attrib,). (1580). *Li sette dolori del Mal Francese*. Perugia: Pietroiacomo Petrucci.

Veneziano, Andrea. (c.1560). *Purgatorio delle cortigiane di Roma. Con un lamento di una Cortigiana che fu favorita poi venuta in calamità per il mal Francese, si condusse andare in carretta*. Rome.

Verini, Giovanni Battista. (1540). *Il Vanto e Lamento della Cortegiana Ferrarese*. Siena.

Zambotti, Bernardino. (1928). '*Diario ferrarese dall'anno 1476 al 1504, appendice al Diario Ferrarese dall'anno 1409 sino al 1502 di autori incerti*'. in Giuseppe Pardi, ed., *Rerum Italicarum Scriptores*, XXIV/7. Bologna: Nicola Zanichelli.

Secondary Sources

Alonge, Roberto. (1974). 'Campani, Niccolò detto Lo Strascino', in Istituto dell'Enciclopedia italiana, ed., *Dizionario Biografico degli Italiani*. Rome: Istituto della Enciclopedia italiana, 17.

Argenziano, Raffaelle. (2013). 'Giobbe e Lazzaro: Santi, malati e protettori. L'iconografia della lebbra a Siena e nel contado tra il XIII e il XV secolo', in Giuseppina De Sandre Gasperini, Maria Clara Rossi, eds., *Malsani. Lebbra e lebbrosi nel medioevo, Quaderni di storia religiosa*. Verona: Cierre, 73–117.

Arrizabalaga, Jon. (2005). 'Medical responses to the "French Disease" in Europe at the turn of the sixteenth century', in Kevin Siena, ed., *Sins of the Flesh*. Toronto: Toronto University Press, 33–55.

Arrizabalaga, Jon, John Henderson, Roger K. French. (1997). *The Great Pox: The French Disease in Renaissance Europe*. New Haven: Yale University Press.

Bailey, Gauvin, Pamela Jones, Franco Mormando, Thomas Worcester, eds. (2005). *Hope and Healing: Painting in Italy in a Time of Plague, 1500–1800*. Chicago: Chicago University Press.

Barker, Sheila. (2021). 'Painting the Plague, 1259–1630', in Christos Lynteris, ed., *Plague Image and Imagination from Medieval to Modern Times*. Basingstoke: Palgrave Macmillan, 37–67. https://research-portal.st-andrews.ac.uk/en/researchoutput/plague-image-and-imagination-from-medieval-to-modern-times(92118270-34f9-4261-aeda-6ae154af6f4e).html.

Barlozzini, Maria Paola (2009). 'Scene di vita medica. MS BAP, G 61 (fine del XVI secolo – inizi del XVII secolo)', in Carla Frova, Ferdinando Treggiari, Maria Alessandra Panzanelli Fratoni, eds. *scheda 36: in Maestri insegnanti e libri a Perugia. Contributi per la storia dell'Università (1308–2008)*, Perugia: Skira, 114–115, 128–9.

Bartoli Langeli, Artilio, Alessandra Panzanelli Fratoni. (2006). *L'invenzione della Biblioteca, Prospero Podiani, Perugia e l'Augusta*, exh. Catalogue. Perugia: Deputazione di Storia Patria per l'Umbria.

Bell, Margaret. (2021). 'On display: Poverty as infirmity and its visual representation at the hospital of Santa Maria della Scala in Siena', in John Henderson, Fredrika Jacobs, Jonathan K. Nelson, eds., *Representing Infirmity*, ch. 4. London: Routledge.

Berco, Cristian. (2016). *From Body to Community: Venereal disease and society in Baroque Spain*. Toronto, University of Toronto Press.

Berco, Cristian. (2011). 'Syphilis, sex and marriage in early modern Spain', *Journal of Early Modern History* 15.3, 223–53.

Bergamini, Giuseppe, Dino Barattini. (2000). *Pellegrino da San Daniele (1467–1547)*. Udine: Forum.

Bertoloni Meli, Domenico. (2017). *Visualizing Disease: The Art and History of Pathological Illustrations*. Chicago: Chicago University Press.

Bindman, David. (1981, 2021). *Hogarth*. London: Thames and Hudson.

Boeckl, Christine M. (2011). *Images of Leprosy: Disease, Religion, and Politics in European Art*. Kirksville: Truman State University Press.

Bourne, Molly. (2008). *Francesco II Gonzaga: The Soldier-Prince as Patron*. Rome: Bulzoni.

Brancher, Dominique. (2015). 'Pox pain and redeeming narratives in Renaissance Europe', in Franziska Gygaz, Miriam Locher, eds., *Narrative Matters in Medical Contexts across Disciplines*. Amsterdam: John Benjamins, 47–69.

Calvi, Giulia. (2022). *The World in Dress: Costume Books across Italy, Europe and the East*. Cambridge: Cambridge University Press.

Carmichael, Ann G. (1990). 'Syphilis and the Columbian exchange: Was the disease really new?', in Mário Gomes Marques, John Cule, eds., *The Great Maritime Discoveries and World Health*. Lisbon: Ecola Nacional de Saude Publica, 187–200.

Carnevale, Laura. (2015). 'Dalla figura di Giobbe alla medicina contemporanea: Per una riflessione su malattia e stigma', *Temp(i)o della sofferenza, temp(i)o di Dio*, *Studi bitontini*, 99–100, 155–67.

Carnevale, Laura. (2010). *Giobbe dall'antichità al medioevo: Testi, tradizioni, immagini*. Bari: Edipuglia.

Cavallo, Sandra, Tessa Storey, eds. (2017). *Conserving Health in Early Modern Culture: Bodies and Environments in Italy and England*. Manchester: Manchester University Press.

Cavallo, Sandra, Tessa Storey. (2013). *Healthy Living in Late Renaissance Italy*. Oxford: Oxford University Press.

Ciccarella, Erica. (2018–19). 'Per una storia del mal francese nel Rinascimento italiano. Tra letteratura e medicina (1494–1629)', Unpublished PhD thesis, Università degli studi di Trento.

Cohn, Samuel K., Jr. (2018). *Epidemics: Hate and Compassion from the Plague of Athens to AIDS*. Oxford: Oxford University Press.

De Angelis, Pietro. (1955). *L'arcispedale di San Giacomo in Augusta*. Rome: Edizioni Italia.

De Ferrari, Augusto. (1988). 'Giovanni Della Croce', in Istituto della Enciclopedia Italiana, ed., *Dizionario Biografico degli Italiani*. Rome: Istituto della Enciclopedia italiana, 36, 796–8.

Eamon, William. (1998). 'Cannibalism and contagion: Framing Syphilis in counter-reformation Italy', *Early Science and Medicine* 3, 1–31.

Fabricius, Johannes. (1994). *Syphilis in Shakespeare's England*. London: Jessica Kingsley.

Falcucci, Gianluca. (2020). *La sifilide a Napoli nel tardo Quattrocento*. Naples: Laboratorio dell'ISPF, XVII.

Foa, Anna. (1990). 'The new and the old: The spread of syphilis (1494–1530)', in Edwin Muir, Guido Ruggiero, eds., *Sex and Gender in Historical Perspective*. Baltimore: Johns Hopkins University Press, 26–45.

French, Roger K. (1985). 'Berengario da Carpi and the use of commentary in anatomical teaching', in Andrew Wear, Roger K. French, Ian M. Lonie, eds., *The Medical Renaissance of the Sixteenth Century*. Cambridge: Cambridge University Press, 42–74.

Frova, Carla, Ferdinando Treggiari, Maria Alessandra Panzanelli Fratoni, eds. (2009). *Maestri insegnanti e libri a Perugia. Contributi per la storia dell'Università (1308–2008)*. Perugia: Skira.

Gagné, John. (2024, forthcoming). 'Lo Strascino's *Lamento* and the Visual Culture of the French Pox around 1500'.

Gardner, Elizabeth E., Federico Zeri. (1971). *Italian Paintings: A Catalogue of the Collection of The Metropolitan Museum of Art: Florentine School*. New York: New York Graphic Society.

Gentilcore, David. (2005). 'Charlatans, the regulated marketplace and the treatment of venereal disease in Italy', in Kevin Siena, ed., *Sins of the Flesh*, ch. 2. Toronto: Toronto University Press.

Gentilcore, David. (2006). *Medical Charlatanism in Early Modern Italy*. Oxford: Oxford University Press.

Geschwind, Rachel. (2012). 'The printed penitent: Magdalene imagery and prostitution reform in early modern Italian chapbooks and broadsheets', in Michelle Erhardt, Amy Morris, eds., *Mary Magdalene, Iconographic Studies from the Middle Ages to the Baroque*. Leiden: Brill, 107–33.

Graf, Arturo. (1888). *Attraverso il Cinquecento*. Turin: Loescher.

Green, Monica H. (2001). *Women's Healthcare in the Medieval West: Texts and Contexts*. Aldershot: Ashgate.

Healy, Margaret. (2001). *Fictions of Disease in Early Modern England: Bodies, Plagues and Politics*. Basingstoke: Palgrave Macmillan.

Helas, Philine. (2018). '" … und sie bekundeten ihm ihre Teilnahme und trösteten ihn wegen all des Unglücks … ". Die Hiobsgeschichte in der italienischen Malerei des 14. und 15. Jahrhunderts' in Thomas Labbé, Gerrit J. Schenk, eds., *Une histoire du sensible: la perception des victims de catastrophe du xiie au xviiie siècle*. Turnhout: Brepols, 69–102.

Henderson, John. (2006). 'Fracastoro, Mal Francese e la cura con il Legno Santo', in Alessandro Pastore, Enrico Peruzzi, eds., *Girolamo Fracastoro: Fra medicina, filosofia e scienze della natura*. Florence: Leo S. Olschki, 73–89.

Henderson, John. (2013). 'Coping with Plagues in renaissance Italy', in Linda Clark, Carole Rawcliffe, eds., *Society in an Age of Plague, The Fifteenth Century*, XII. Woodbridge: Boydell Press, 175–94.

Henderson, John. (2021a). 'Die bildliche Darstellung der Franzosenkrankheit im frühneuzeitlichen Italien: Patienten, Krankheitsbild und Behandlung', in Michael Stolberg, ed., *Körper-Bilder in der Frühen Neuzeit. Kunst-, medizin- und mediengeschichtliche Perspektiven*. Munich: De Gruyter Oldenbourg, 15–35.

Henderson, John. (2021b). 'Representing infirmity in early modern Florence', in John Henderson, Fredrika Jacobs, Jonathan K. Nelson, eds., *Representing Infirmity*. London: Routledge, 47–67.

Henderson, John, Fredrika Jacobs, Jonathan K. Nelson, eds. (2020). *Representing Infirmity in Renaissance and Early Modern Europe*. London: Routledge.

Hewlett, Mary. (2005) 'The French connection: Syphilis and Sodomy in late renaissance Lucca', in Kevin Siena, ed., *Sins of the Flesh*, ch. 9. Toronto: Toronto University Press, 239–60.

Jacquart, Danielle, Claude Thomasset. (1985). *Sexuality and Medicine in the Middle Ages*. Oxford: Polity.

James, Carolyn. (2020). *A Renaissance Marriage: The Political and Personal Alliance of Isabella d'Este and Francesco Gonzaga 1490–1519*. Oxford: Oxford University Press.

Kinzelbach, Annemarie, Monika Weber. (2022). *Steinreich – das Schneidhaus der Fugger in Augsburg*. Deutsches Medizinhistorisches Museum: Ingolstadt.

Kunzle, David. (1973). *The Early Comic Strip; Narrative Strips and Picture Stories in the European Broadsheet from c.1450 to 1825*. Berkeley: University of California Press.

Kurz, Hilde. (1952). 'Italian models of Hogarth's picture stories', *Journal of the Warburg and Courtauld Institutes* 15.3–4, 136–68.

Kusukawa, Sachiko. (2012). *Picturing the Book of Nature: Image, Text, and Argument in Sixteenth-Century Human Anatomy and Medical Botany*. Chicago: Chicago University Press.

Leong, Elaine. (2008). 'Making medicines in the early modern household', *Bulletin of the History of Medicine* 82, 145–68.

Lodone, Michele. (2015). 'San Giobbe nell'Italia del Rinascimento: Le dimensioni di una devozione', *Rivista di Storia e Letteratura Religiosa* LI.1, 3–56.

Losse, Deborah N. (2015). *Medicine, Metaphor, and Religious Conflict in Early Modern France*. Columbus: Ohio State University.

Lucco, Mauro. (1990). *Pinacoteca di Brera, Scuola Veneta*, ed., Federico Zeri. Milan: Electra.

Lupi, Regina. (2014). 'L'Università di Perugia in età moderna: Una dialettica tra stato e corporazioni urbane', *Annali di storia delle università italiane* 18, 185–93.

Maovaz, Marco, Ileana Giambanco, Rosario Francesco Donato, Bruno Romano. (2008). 'La medicina nell'Università di Perugia', *Annali della Facoltà di Medicina e Chirurgia*, Università di Perugia, 96–8.

Matthews Grieco, Sara F. (1997). 'Pedagogical Prints', in Geraldine A. Johnson, Sara F. Matthews Grieco, eds., *Picturing Women in Renaissance and Baroque Italy*. Cambridge: Cambridge University Press, 61–87.

McGough, Laura J. (2011). *Gender, Sexuality and Syphilis in Early Modern Venice: The Disease that Came to Stay*. Basingstoke: Palgrave Macmillan.

McGough, Laura J. (2005). 'Quarantining beauty: The French disease in early renaissance Venice', in Kevin Siena, ed., *Sins of the Flesh*, ch. 8. Toronto: Toronto University Press, 211–38.

Munger, Robert S. (1949). 'Guaiacum, the holy wood from the new world', *Journal of the History of Medicine and the Allied Sciences* 4.1, 196–229.

Niccoli, Ottavia. (1990). *Prophecy and People in Renaissance Italy*, trans., Lydia G. Cochrane. Princeton: Princeton University Press.

Novelli, Maria Angela. (2008). *Scarsellino*. Milan: Skira.

Nutton, Vivian. (2004). *Ancient Medicine*. London: Routledge.

Nutton, Vivian. (1983). 'The seeds of disease: An explanation of contagion and infection from the Greeks to the Renaissance', *Medical History* 27.1, 1–34

O'Brien, Monica C. (2019). 'Contagion, morality and practicality: The French pox in Frankfurt am Main and Nuremberg, 1495–1700', University of Glasgow, PhD thesis.

Panzanelli Fratoni, Alessandra. (2012). 'Prospero Podiani (ca. 1535–1615) and the foundation of a city library', *Italian Studies Library Group Bulletin*, 36–43.

Pelling, Margaret. (1986). 'Appearance and reality: Barber-surgeons, the body and disease', in A. L. Beier, Roger Finlay, eds., *The Making of the Metropolis: London, 1500–1700*, ch. 3. Harlow: Longmans, 82–112.

Pelling, Margaret, Frances White. (2003). *Medical Conflicts in Early Modern London. Patronage, Physicians, and Irregular Practitioners 1550–1640*. Oxford: Oxford University Press.

Peruzzi, Enrico. (1997). 'Gerolamo Fracastoro', in Istituto della Enciclopedia Italiana, ed., *Dizionario Biografico degli Italiani*. Rome: Istituto della Enciclopedia italiana, 49, 544.

Pieri, Marzia. (2010). *Lo Strascino da Siena e la sua opera poetica e teatrale*. Pisa: ETS.

Pomata, Gianna. (1998). *Contracting a Cure: Patients, Healers and the Law in Early Modern Bologna*. Baltimore: Johns Hopkins University Press.

Presciutti, Diana Bullen. (2021). 'The Friar as medico: Picturing Leprosy, Institutional Care, and Franciscan Virtues in *La Franceschina*', in John Henderson, Fredrika Jacobs, Jonathan K. Nelson, eds., *Representing Infirmity*, ch. 5. London: Routledge, 93–116.

Puccinotti, Francesco. (1850–66). *Storia della medicina*, ii/2. Livorno: Wagner Editore.

Pullan, Brian S. (2016). *Tolerance, Regulation and Rescue: Dishonoured Women and Abandoned Children in Italy, 1300–1800*. Manchester: Manchester University Press.

Qualtiere, Louis F., William E. Slights. (2003). 'Contagion and blame in early modern England: The case of the French Pox', *Literature and Medicine* 22.1, 1–24.

Quétel, Claude. (1990). *History of Syphilis*. Oxford: Polity Press.

Raimond-Waarts, Loes L., Catrien Santing. (2010). 'Sex: A cardinal's sin. Punished by Syphilis in renaissance Rome', *Leidschrift* 25, 169–82.

Rawcliffe, Carole. (2006). *Leprosy in Medieval England*. Woodbridge: Boydell.

Rosenthal, Margaret F. (1992). *The Honest Courtesan: Veronica Franco. Citizen and Writer in Sixteenth-Century Venice.* Chicago: Chicago University Press.

Rublack, Ulinka. (2010). *Dressing up: Cultural Identity in Renaissance Europe.* Oxford: Oxford University Press.

Russsell, Paul A. (1989). 'Syphilis, God's scourge or nature's vengeance? The German printed response to a public problem in the early sixteenth century', *Archiv für Reformationsgeschichte* 80, 286–307.

Salmon, Marylynn. (2022). *Medieval Syphilis and Treponemal Disease.* New York: ARC Humanities Press.

Salzberg, Rosa. (2010). 'In the mouth of charlatans: Street performers and the dissemination of pamphlets in Renaissance Italy', *Renaissance Studies* 24. 5, 638–53.

Sampson, Lisa. (2024, forthcoming). 'Performance in music and on stage', in Guyda Armstrong, Rhiannon Daniels, Catherine Keen, eds., *Cambridge History of Poetry in Italy 1200–1600.* Cambridge: Cambridge University Press.

Schleiner, William. (1993). 'Infection and cure through women: Renaissance constructions of the French disease', *Journal of Medieval and Renaissance Studies* 24.3, 499–517.

Schleiner, William. (1994). 'Moral attitudes toward syphilis and its prevention in the Renaissance', *Bulletin of the History of Medicine* 68, 389–410.

Shaw, James, Evelyn Welch. (2011). *Making Medicine in Renaissance Florence.* Amsterdam: Ridopi.

Shemek, Deanna. (1998). *Ladies Errant: Wayward Women and Social Order in Early Modern Italy.* Durham: Duke University Press.

Shemek, Deanna. (2004). '"Mi mostrano a ditto tutti quanti": Disease, diexis and disfiguration in the *Lamento di una cortigiana ferrarese*', in Paul A. Ferrara, Eugenio L. Giusti, Jane Tylus, eds., *Italiana* XI: *Medusa's Gaze: Essays on Gender, Literature, and Aesthetics in Honor of Robert J. Rodini.* Indiana: Bordighera, 49–64.

Siena, Kevin. (1998). 'Pollution, promiscuity and the pox: English venereology and the early modern medical discourse on social and sexual danger', *Journal of the History of Sexuality* 8.4, 553–74.

Siena, Kevin, ed. (2005). *Sins of the Flesh: Responding to Sexual Disease in Early Modern Europe.* Toronto: Toronto University Press.

Siena, Kevin. (2005). 'The clean and the foul: Paupers and the pox in London hospitals, c.1550–c.1700', in Kevin Siena, ed., *Sins of the Flesh*, ch. 10. Toronto: Toronto University Press, 261–84.

Siraisi, Nancy. (1990). *Medieval and Early Renaissance Medicine: An Introduction to Knowledge and Practice.* Chicago: Chicago University Press.

Stein, Claudia. (2009). *Negotiating the French Pox in Early Modern Germany.* London: Routledge.

Stein, Claudia. (2006). 'The meaning of signs: Diagnosing the French pox in early modern Augsburg', *Bulletin of the History of Medicine* 80.4, 617–48.

Stroppiana, Luigi. (1968). *Storia dell'Ospedale di S. Maria della Misericordia e S. Nicolò degli incurabili in Perugia.* Perugia: Grafica.

Stolberg, Michael. (2021). 'Epilogue: Did Mona Lisa suffer from hypothyroidism? Visual representations of sickness and the vagaries of retrospective diagnosis', in John Henderson, Fredrika Jacobs, Jonathan K. Nelson, eds., *Representing Infirmity*, ch. 11. London: Routledge. 233–47.

Storey, Tessa. (2008). *Carnal Commerce in Counter-Reformation Rome.* Cambridge: Cambridge University Press.

Strocchia, Sharon T. (2019). *Forgotten Healers: Women and the Pursuit of Health in Late Renaissance Italy.* Cambridge, MA: Harvard University Press.

Strocchia, Sharon T., Ryan Kelly. (2022). 'Picturing the pox in Italian popular prints, 1550–1650', *Renaissance Studies* 36.5, 723–49.

Terrien, Samuel. (1996). *The Iconography of Job through the Centuries: Artists as Biblical Interpreters.* Pennsylvania: Pennsylvania State University Press.

Tognotti, Eugenia. (2006). *L'altra faccia di Venere: La sifilide dalla prima età moderna all'avvento dell'Aids (XV-XX secc).* Milan: Franco Angeli.

Tosti, Antonio. (1992). *Storie all'ombra del malfrancese.* Palermo: Sellerio Editore.

Ugolini, Paola. (2009). 'The Satirist's Purgatory: *Il Purgatorio delle Cortegiane* and the writer's discontent', *Italian Studies* 64.1, 1–19.

Wear, Andrew. (2000). *Knowledge and Practice in English Medicine, 1550–1680.* Cambridge: Cambridge University Press.

Wilson, Bronwen. (2005). *The World in Venice: Print, the City, and Early Modern Identity.* Toronto: Toronto University Press.

Winterbottom, Anna E. (2015). 'Of the China root: A case study of the early modern circulation of *Materia Medica*', *Social History of Medicine* 28.1, 22–44.

Zanca, Attilio. (1974). 'Il Mal Francese', *Kos* 1.1, 77–92.

Zanobio, Bruno, Giuseppe Armocida. (1983). 'Alfonso Corradi', in Istituto della Enciclopedia Italiana, ed., *Dizionario Biografico degli Italiani*. Rome: Istituto della enciclopedia italiana.

Zanré, Daniele . (2005). 'French diseases and Italian responses: Representations of the Mal Francese in the literature of cinquecento Tuscany', in Kevin Siena, ed., *Sins of the Flesh*, Toronto: Toronto University Press, 187–208.

Acknowledgements

I am very grateful to Jonathan Nelson and Sheilagh Ogilvie and the external readers for their invaluable comments on earlier drafts, and to Flavia Manservigi for her meticulous checking of translations. I should also like to thank those who have helped me in many ways with the images reproduced here, including Sabrina Minuzzi and Gaston Javier Basile, and Julia Biel of the Fototeca of the Kunsthistorisches Institut in Florence. I have much benefitted from discussions with many people about the Perugian album of watercolours, including Maria Pia Donato, Chris Fischer, Jack Hartnell, Peter Jones, Annemarie Kinzelbach, Alessandra Panzanelli Fratoni, Carole Rawcliffe and Pat Rubin. I am very grateful to colleagues at the Biblioteca Augusta in Perugia, especially dott'a Francesca Grauso and dott. Paolo Renzi, for information about Podiani and his library, and to Regina Lupi for her knowledgeable and very helpful advice in Perugia.

The Renaissance

John Henderson
Birkbeck, University of London, and Wolfson College, University of Cambridge

John Henderson is Emeritus Professor of Italian Renaissance History at Birkbeck, University of London, and Emeritus Fellow of Wolfson College, University of Cambridge. His recent publications include *Florence Under Siege: Surviving Plague in an Early Modern City* (2019), *Plague and the City*, edited with Lukas Engelmann and Christos Lynteris (2019), and *Representing Infirmity: Diseased Bodies in Renaissance Italy*, edited with Fredrika Jacobs and Jonathan K. Nelson (2021). He is also the author of *Piety and Charity in Late Medieval Florence* (1994); *The Great Pox: The French Disease in Renaissance Europe*, with Jon Arrizabalaga and Roger French (1997); and *The Renaissance Hospital: Healing the Body and Healing the Soul* (2006). Forthcoming publications include a Cambridge Element, *Representing and Experiencing the Great Pox in Renaissance Italy* (2024).

Jonathan K. Nelson
Syracuse University Florence

Jonathan K. Nelson teaches Italian Renaissance Art at Syracuse University Florence and is research associate at the Harvard Kennedy School. His books include *Filippino Lippi* (2004, with Patrizia Zambrano); *Leonardo e la reinvenzione della figura femminile* (2007), *The Patron's Payoff: Conspicuous Commissions in Italian Renaissance Art* (2008, with Richard J. Zeckhauser), *Filippino Lippi* (2022); and he co-edited *Representing Infirmity. Diseased Bodies in Renaissance Italy* (2021). He co-curated museum exhibitions dedicated to Michelangelo (2002), Botticelli and Filippino (2004), Robert Mapplethorpe (2009), and Marcello Guasti (2019), and two online exhibitions about Bernard Berenson (2012, 2015). Forthcoming publications include a Cambridge Element, *Risks in Renaissance Art: Production, Purchase, Reception* (2023).

Assistant Editor
Sarah McBryde, *Birkbeck, University of London*

Editorial Board
Wendy Heller, *Scheide Professor of Music History, Princeton University*
Giorgio Riello, *Chair of Early Modern Global History, European University Institute, Florence*
Ulinka Rublack, *Professor of Early Modern History, St Johns College, University of Cambridge*
Jane Tylus, *Andrew Downey Orrick Professor of Italian and Professor of Comparative Literature, Yale University*

About the Series
Timely, concise, and authoritative, Elements in the Renaissance showcases cutting-edge scholarship by both new and established academics. Designed to introduce students, researchers, and general readers to key questions in current research, the volumes take multi-disciplinary and transnational approaches to explore the conceptual, material, and cultural frameworks that structured Renaissance experience.

Cambridge Elements $\equiv$

The Renaissance

A full series listing is available at: www.cambridge.org/EREN

Printed in the United States
by Baker & Taylor Publisher Services